The Devil, You Say!

Doubleday books by Andrew M. Greeley

AND YOUNG MEN SHALL SEE VISIONS

THE CATHOLIC EXPERIENCE

COME BLOW YOUR MIND WITH ME

THE DEVIL, YOU SAY!

THE FRIENDSHIP GAME

A FUTURE TO HOPE IN

THE HESITANT PILGRIM

THE JESUS MYTH

LETTERS TO NANCY

LIFE FOR A WANDERER

THE NEW AGENDA

PRIESTS IN THE UNITED STATES:
Reflections on a Survey

THE SINAI MYTH

The Devil, You Say!

MAN AND HIS PERSONAL DEVILS AND ANGELS

BY

ANDREW M. GREELEY

1974

DOUBLEDAY & COMPANY, INC.
GARDEN CITY, NEW YORK

BJ
1401
.G73

Library of Congress Cataloging in Publication Data

Greeley, Andrew M.   1928–
  The Devil, you say!

  1. Good and evil.   I. Title.
BJ1401.G73   917.3'03'92
ISBN 0-385-08789-6
Library of Congress Catalog Card Number 74-7898

Contents

6   *Contents*

The Devil, You Say!

Introduction

Charles Meyer has recently suggested that we are moving from an age of the mystadelic to an age of the mystagogic. We have tried for a century and a half to explain away all mysteries. It hasn't worked too well. Now we are moving toward a more reverential attitude about the mysterious. We are prepared to concede with some humility that there are many things we do not understand and some that we will never understand. The ecological and environmental movement has forcefully made the point that many of our current problems come from a mistaken belief that humankind is the master of the physical world and can do anything to and with that world he wants. But the intellectual origins of our arrogant self-image as master of the universe are to be found in an even more dangerous form of hubris by which we conceptualized ourselves as the intellectual lords of the universe. We could do anything we wanted to the world because we knew everything there was to know about it. There may have been a mystery here or there—cure for cancer, for example—but we were serenely confident that science, rationality, secularity and democratic liberalism would tidy up the remaining messy puzzles in short order.

This Enlightenment self-confidence is moribund. It may still receive some lip service from an older generation of scientists and journalists, but lots of people never bought it to begin with. (Astrology was a multimillion-dollar business long before the universities discovered it.) The younger generation of the intellectual elite have decisively abandoned it in favor of something rather like Professor Roszak's new Gnosticism. Mystery, in short, is "in."

Catholics, of course, seem to be always the last to catch up. We abandoned the mysterious just about the time the counterculture was discovering it. For the last century or so, we have been very defensive about mystery. We were told as children that a mystery was something we had to believe, under pain of mortal sin, whether we understood it or not. Still, our catechisms did their best to explain the mysteries. There was always the undigestible lump in the mysteries of the Trinity and the Incarnation, and we knew that no one would ever be able to give a completely satisfactory explanation. But we could continue to peel away the layers of mystery in the hope that someday the explanation would be so good that the final residue of mystery would be no problem for anyone.

Mystery, then, was an obstacle, a test, a difficulty to be overcome; it was an unfortunate but necessary impediment to faith, an embarrassment in dealing with non-Catholics, toward whom the answers of apologetic Catholicism were directed. (And that we never encountered anyone in the real world who asked those questions we were prepared to answer seemed unimportant.)

Such was the mystadelic style, the style of the Enlightenment, the style of explaining away the mysterious. The mystagogue approaches mystery from a completely different perspective. Mystery is not a puzzle to be solved, an answer to be given, a problem to be explained away, an embarrassment to be eliminated. Mystery is rather a secret to be revealed. The mystagogue is not interested in "understanding"; he is committed to probing secrets so that more about the meaning of reality and the meaning of human life may be revealed to him. For the mystagogic Catholic, the Trinity and the Incarnation are not awkward puzzles to be believed under pain of mortal sin but illuminations revealing great secrets about the nature of the universe and the destiny of human life. The mystagogue seeks to know more about the mysteries. He does not seek for rational explanations of them, rather to learn from them how to live, how to be in harmony with the basic powers that underpin the universe. The mystadelic may be interested in theoretical debates, in scientific journals, in theological manuals, and in catechetical instruction classes. The mystagogue is eminently practical; he wants to know how to live and turns to the illumination of the mysteries, to the light that comes from secrets revealed, in order to find practical, concrete insights about how one should live. The theoretical physicist who is also an astrologer (and such people are relatively numerous on the university campuses today) has blended the mystagogic and mystadelic dimensions of human life.

There is in the mystagogic approach a conviction that some things are "natural." Certain kinds of behavior are "harmonious"; they fit in with the right order of things, and if one learns the "secrets," one can live a life of "natural harmony." Transcendental meditation, the natural food movement, and devotion to the I Ching are all manifestations of the quest for the "natural." Wilson Carey McWilliams, in his brilliant study *The Idea of Fraternity in America,* observes that quotation marks appear around the word "nature" much less frequently than they did just a few years ago. In the Enlightenment perspective "nature" was a power to be conquered and brought under control. In the post-Enlightenment world nature is a system of forces to be respected and with which to harmonize one's behavior. McWilliams points out that it is but a step from taking the quotation marks away from nature to acknowledging the existence of a law of nature or "natural law." The new Gnostics, the counterculturists, the devotees of Eastern religion, the natural food enthusiasts are all (although they perhaps would not be explicit about it) seeking to know nature's law and to live by it. Catholicism scores once again: we abandoned natural law just when others were discovering it.

The mystagogue, then, searches through the secrets of mystery in order that he might discover the laws of nature and by following them live a happy and harmonious life. The change from the mystadelic to the mystagogic, described by such diverse authors as Meyer, Roszak, and McWilliams, is surely one of the most important cultural phenomena of our time. It is also a change that requires a severe wrenching of perspective for those of us who were raised in the view of apologetic Catholicism and considered ourselves to be liberated from that view by the second Vatican Council. We finally made it into the Enlightenment just as that two-century-old cultural phenomenon expired. God didn't die in the middle 1960s but the Enlightenment did. We liberated American Catholics are sitting around at its wake wondering where the hell everyone else is. Occasionally we ask whether we ought to move back to the rectory basement for a discussion of a chapter of Father Farrel's *Companion to the Summa*. But the return to mystery is not a return to such nostalgic things as benediction or the Sorrowful Mother novena; it is a return to an attitude, a world view, that was left behind several centuries before 1960. Paradoxically enough, in our battle against the Enlightenment we seem to have taken on many of the worst modes of thought that characterized that bitter cultural enemy of ours. There are, as my colleague Peter Rossi used to remark, many ironies in the fire.

Of course, one does not write off centuries of scientific progress (despite Professor Roszak and his disciples); one does not reject rationality (despite Norman O. Brown and his disciples); one does not abandon the wisdom of the past in confidence of better wisdom in the future (despite Margaret Mead and her disciples). The quest for explanation and understanding, on the one hand, and the probing of secret and mystery on the other need not be in conflict with one another. Quite the contrary, as Edward Tiryakian has pointed out, a more typical situation is one in which the scientists and Gnostics are the same people.[1] The quest for knowledge and the quest for wisdom seem incompatible to us only because of the special cultural situation that has existed for the last several centuries. We may have to go through a period when science is abandoned in favor of wisdom, but hope-

[1] Edward Tiryakian, "Toward the Sociology of Esoteric Culture," *American Journal of Sociology*, 78, 3 (November 1972), pp. 491–511.

fully the period will be short, and we will rediscover the truths known by our ancestors in the sixteenth and thirteenth centuries: science and wisdom desperately need each other.

I hope to write a book about reverence, which I take to be the appropriate Christian response to contemporary humankind's rediscovery of nature. In this volume I intend something relatively more modest. I want to explore some aspects of the mystery of evil.

There are three great mysteries: the mystery of being, the mystery of the unity of being, and the mystery of evil. The first is not why there is a world or whether there is a God; it is much more profound than that. It is the mystery of why there is anything at all. Given contingent beings, it follows logically that there must be a necessary being. But why is there being in the first place? How come there is anything? It is not a question that too many people ponder, although all the creation myths developed throughout the history of humankind are attempts to cope with the question. It is an issue that is tolerable when it is presented in symbolic language, but when it is stated in blunt unadorned prose, "How come there is anything?", the question gives one a headache in about fifteen minutes.

The second question baffled the Greeks and all philosophers who read them. It is the question of the one and the many, of unity and diversity, homogeneity and heterogeneity. Which is more real, which is more ultimate, the one or the many? Does the one exist only in and through the many? Or do the many exist only and through the one? Most of the social symbols that humankind has developed deal with this problem. The clan, the tribe, totemic groups, and, in more recent times, the nation and the state are all images and pictures developed so that humans can cope with the puzzle of unity and diversity as they experience it in their political and social lives. The symbols of the Trinity and the Incarnation are religious and theological images devoted to the same problem.

The third of the great mysteries is the problem of the struggle between being, which is good, and non-being, which is evil. Why is being trapped in combat with non-being? Why is good apparently in bondage to evil? Why does evil appear to be perpetually on the verge of overwhelming good? Why do we experience in our own persons and in the social and physical cosmos this constant desperate struggle between good and evil, life and death, love and hatred, being and non-being?

Note well that the mystery of evil is not quite the same thing as the problem of evil. (And this is *not* one more book about the problem of evil.) The "problem" is to a considerable extent an Enlightenment issue, although of course the question was raised long before the Enlightenment. It usually goes something like this: You claim God is good, but there is evil in the world. But since God is the cause of everything in the world, therefore God is the cause of evil. Therefore you are wrong.

In only slightly more elaborate form one can find the same argument in college philosophy textbooks and in the scholarly treatises of atheistic philosophers. There is always a tone of smug, realistic, self-satisfaction at the end of the argument. The point has been made, it is irrefutable; there is evil in the world, and therefore there can be no God. There are ways, of course, that the argument can be answered on logical grounds. The most radical of the responses is that of the philosopher Charles Hartshorne, a disciple of Alfred North Whitehead. I find the Whitehead-Hartshorne notion of a pragmatic, flexible, "play-it-by-ear" God rather attractive. Perhaps such a deity appeals to my Irish pragmatic political disposition. In any case, if the reader wants to deal with the problem of evil, Whitehead and Hartshorne (and Father Capon's popular version) make a good beginning place.

But I have always felt that we make a mistake to argue with those who raise the problem of evil. Let them spin out their syllogism, let them make their case, and be prepared to concede their conclusion. Then say to them, "What comes next?" Having "proved" satisfactorily that there is no God, what do they have to say about the conflict between good and evil, which they must perceive is in the world and in their own personalities? Having used evil to explain away ultimate Good, how do they explain ordinary good and the struggle between it and plain, ordinary evil? What insight and wisdom does their syllogism provide for the puzzles and mysteries of human living? Maybe, just maybe, there are things going on in the universe that their deep, logical constructs have missed; maybe there are secrets still to be discovered, voyages of exploration still to be undertaken, wisdom still to be acquired. What, then, comes next?

This book, however, is not about the problem of evil. I do not want to engage in dialectics on the existence of God with those who are still fixated on the questions that college sophomores asked in the Enlightenment era. I wish to deal with the mystery of evil, and, more especially, with the mystery of human evil. It seems that we are trapped. The good we wish to do we fail to do, and the evil we wish to avoid is just what we do too frequently. Conflict between good and evil threatens to tear our personalities apart, and it is the most practically pressing of the three great mysteries. I surely do not propose to solve the mystery or even to make a definitive exploration of it. In principle I believe that neither exercise is possible. What I intend to do in in this book is to explore some of the traps in which we are caught, some of the bonds of evil that restrict our freedom to be good, some of the conflicts that war within our personalities, some of the devils that dominate and frustrate our existence.

Make no mistake, we are each of us trapped. Even the person who announces bravely (perhaps after a nude encounter marathon) that he or she is at last free is still trapped. If nothing else, he is now caught in the need to proclaim his own freedom. We are engaged in constant conflict with demons. They bind us, restrain us, trick us and trap us. They are demons which stem from our genetic limitations and our physical frailties—sickness, weariness, discouragement. There are other demons that arise from the limitations of our social class, our ethnic background, our cultural milieu; and there are yet others that play on the weaknesses that we have acquired in our childhood and adolescent experiences. The most powerful of all the demons, of course, is that which torments us because we hunger to be everything and we are limited. The ultimate trap we are caught in results from being a finite creature seeking the Infinite, a relative creature seeking the Absolute, a limited creature aspiring to the universal.

In the next chapter I shall explore the devil symbol, a not unreasonable attempt to explain the extraordinary power of evil. The various traps of evil are so clever, and the various chains of evil are so strong that on the face of it it does not seem absurd to consider the possibility that there is an evil genius at work. The evil in our personalities is authentically diabolic. That during the third and fourth decades of the twentieth century two of the most powerful nations on earth were presided over by paranoid madmen seems too much to be attibuted to chance. Furthermore, as we have learned more about how bland and dull the personalities of Hitler and Stalin were, we are appalled and astonished that such trivial men could create such unspeakable suffering. Hannah Arendt's point about the banality of evil as personified in Adolph Eichmann might well lead one to conclude that behind the banality is an incredibly fiendish design. If there is a plot, there must be a plotter.

This book is about modern devils, though most of them I will describe have been around for a long time. They have simply donned new clothes so as to keep up with the latest fashion. Not so long ago one would have to insist that the devils were really only weaknesses of the human personality and the human social system, for there was no such thing as personal evil spirits lurking outside of the individual person or society. No intelligent, enlightened person took seriously the possibility that the devil symbol might represent another reality beyond psychic or social malfunctions. I am no longer quite so sure about that. Unquestionably, the demons I describe in this book do represent frailties, proclivities, tendencies, inclinations in the personality and in society. They do admit of social-psychological analysis. But to "explain" these devils by the insights of social science provides no answer for why these tendencies exist in the individual and society. We simply do not know why there are such individual and social devils. We are not likely to ever know. To exclude on a priori grounds the possibility of personal devils is as dogmatic as to insist on a priori grounds that such beings exist. I do not want to argue about the subject in this book. There are demons with which we must battle every day, and it is about them that I propose to write. I think in the final analysis that the question of whether these demons have a personal existence of their own is relatively unimportant. What is critical for us is to understand the dynamics of our daily struggles with the principalities and the powers of evil. Demons exist. Anyone with any consciousness of the conflicts raging within himself knows that they do. Whether they are independent personages or not is less important than that we are tormented. Any naïve innocent who thinks that by having rid himself of belief in a personal devil he is free from the daily conflict with his own particular demons is kidding himself.

This book was conceived and written before the bizarre cult of demonology stirred up by *The Exorcist* swept the country. As I hope will be clear from the text, my approach has nothing to do with the cheap, exploitive sensationalism of that third-rate cinematic shocker. It is one of the devil's tricks to hide under the mantle of the occult. As long as he is an "occult phenomenon" causing little girls to do vile things and killing Teilhard-like Jesuits, he need not be taken seriously in the real world of our everyday life. The evil one is greatly pleased when people think his principal threat is possession and black magic.

CHAPTER 1

The Devil, You Say!

In one of his periodic admonitions, Pope Paul VI recently warned the world of the reality of Satan and the evils of Satanism. Though his statement spoke of Satan as a spiritual entity rather than a flesh-and-blood creature stalking the earth, progressive Roman Catholics were acutely embarrassed. An American Catholic Scripture scholar remarked, "No up-to-date theologian believes that Satan is a person." Enlightened secular humanists wrote off the papal warning as one more lamentable Pauline *faux pas*. Asserting the personal reality of Satan was just what one might expect from the man who attempted (unsuccessfully, as it turned out) to prevent Catholics from using the birth control pill. Satan, indeed!

[And yet Anton Szandor La Vey does a land-office business as the high priest of the Church of Satan in San Francisco, where he preaches such satanic commandments as "Satan represents vengeance instead of turning the other cheek," and "Satan represents kindness to those who deserve it instead of love wasted on ingrates," and "Satan represents indulgence instead of abstinence."] Ruth Nanda Anshen, an editor of a number of lofty humanistic publications, has produced a new book called *The Reality of the Devil* from the impeccable secular publishing house of Harper & Row. She concludes her book with a warning from which Paul VI could not dissent: "God's ways and the Devil's way part. There certainly is greatness on each side . . . We may with certainty rely on God or on the Devil. The choice is ours."

Rosemary's Baby and *The Exorcist* are bestsellers. Dennis Wheatley's novels of Satanism are airport paperback-rack favorites. In a cemetery in Florida heads have been stolen from six graves, perhaps to be used in a witches' ceremony. Two men charged with murder recently in Montana and California are reported to have admitted they dismembered their victims as part of a satanic ritual. In Livingston County, Michigan, a seventeen-year-old girl is tortured and slain, and those charged with the killing claim to be "Satan's satanic servants." In New Jersey, newspapers report, Patrick Michael Newell was killed so that he could return to earth as a leader of "40 leagues of demons." Charles Manson periodically claims to be Satan. According to *Time,* one of the "Council of Nine" in La Vey's Church of Satan, a fourth-degree satanic "priest," is also a U. S. Army officer and the author of a "widely used R.O.T.C. textbook." In various suburban basements around the country young marrieds peel off their clothes (thus becoming "sky clad") and jump within a nine-foot circle to celebrate a witches' sabbat. Witches of Britain still claim credit for resisting Hitler's invasion. (They cast a spell across the English Channel.) The British Isles are periodically disturbed by nighttime invasions of graveyards in which graves are desecrated, crosses broken, and coffins opened. Susy Smith, the author of *Today's Witches,* argues that there are sixty thousand witches in the United States, but other "witch specialists" argue there are two hundred thousand. As the mother in *The Exorcist* observes, she's not sure that God exists, but she is sure that Satan does.

If Satan, then, is still in business, it behooves us to be prepared to greet him with proper respect when we encounter him. According to those who have had dealings with him, he is not a being you would have difficulty recognizing the second time around. The Buddhist devil Mara has "hands and feet . . . wrapped in the coils of 100,000 serpents, and in its hands . . . swords, bows, arrows, pikes, axes, mallets, rockets, pestles, sticks, spears, clubs, discuses, and other instruments of war. . . . Its faces glitter in terrible splendor, its dog-teeth are enormous and fearful to behold. . . . Its tongues were as rough as mats of hair, its eyes red and glittering like those of black serpents full of venom."

Pazuzu, the lean, southwest-wind devil of Assyria, has great wings, a huge hook on his head, and an ugly, evil grin on his face. The Gorgons, Greek evil spirits, look much the same, although they are usually modestly dressed in Greek tunics, unlike the naked Pazuzu. Tiamat, the Babylonian goddess of chaos, is a horned and clawed fowl, while Set, her Egyptian counterpart (Typhon to the Greeks) is either a snake or a crocodile.

The Christian Devil tends to be much more human in form; indeed, in some ancient Byzantine paintings, he is presented as a strong, attractive young man—in deference to the Christian tradition that he is a fallen angel. Some Christian artists have portrayed him as a pig, based on a description of St. Anthony, who had frequent tête-à-têtes with his satanic majesty in the desert. However, other artists, such as Goya, Dürer, Bosch, Giotto, favor the billy-goat Devil. Occasionally, as in the case of Goya's famous painting of a sabbat, the Devil is pure billy goat—though of a very sexy and self-satisfied variety. But for other painters he is both goat and human in form, having at all times the horns, the legs and the beard of a goat, frequently the torso of a human being and usually the wings of an angel. It was ancient practice that, when one religion supplanted another, the god of the old became the devil of the new, and this may explain the Christian's goatish Satan. Apparently one of the divine figures of the Celtic and Teutonic northland to be replaced—however incompletely—by the Christian God was a horned deity. From a deity with horns to a devil billy goat was a small step for the Christian imagination.

It may, incidentally, be an exercise in male chauvinism to refer to the Devil as "he." The Gorgons were female, as was their colleague Kali, the black many-armed goddess with a belt of human skulls so popular in folk Hinduism. Occasionally the billy-goat Christian Devil is portrayed with breasts. Some of the contemporary versions of Satanism worship a hermaphroditic Satan. Many of the primitive nature religions also imagine that the principle of disorder and chaos in the world is feminine. The female vulva scratched on cave walls in the late Ice Age may well symbolize a feared evil spirit.

If all of these forms of the Devil would be easily recognized should we meet him (or her, both) crossing Times Square at rush hour, the Satan who visited Ivan Karamazov was less easily recognizable—and hence considerably more frightening:

"He was a gentleman, or rather a peculiarly Russian sort of gentleman . . . going a little grey, with long thick hair and a pointed beard. . . . He looked like one of those landed proprietors who flourished during the days of serfdom; he had lived in good society, but bit by bit, impoverished by his youthful dissipations and the recent abolition of serfdom, he had become a sort of high-class sponger, admitted into the society of his former acquaintances because of his pliable disposition, as a man one need not be ashamed to know, whom one can invite to meet anybody, only fairly far down the table. . . ."

Such a vision of Satan is perfectly in keeping with my fantasy of the Devil comfortably occupying a position as tenured faculty member at a divinity school in the San Francisco Bay area—probably specializing in the theology of revolution. (My alternative fantasy is that he is a gunman for the Irish Republican Army.) In fact, however, everyone knows that the Devil, like God, is French. To tell the truth they are both French Jesuits.

One need not spend much time over the protocol of what the Devil ought to be called. *Satan* in Hebrew means "the accuser" or "the adversary." And when the Hebrew Scriptures were translated into Greek, the word *diabolos* (hence, our "Devil") was used for *Satan*. *Lucifer* or "light bearer" is a name the early Christians frequently used for the Devil. It became popular in the era between the two Testaments and probably represents influence on the Hebrew religion of Iranian dualism. The Iranian's "Prince of Darkness" was called Ahra Manyu or Ahriman. Among the California Indians he is called Coyote. The Algonquin Indians called him Gluskap. In Northern Siberia he is the Great Crow. Other Siberian tribes called him Ngaa. The

Teutons' name for him is Loki, and Loki's daughter Hel is the queen of the world's dead (thus our "hell"). The Celts and the Slavs haven't agreed on very much in human history, but they both called the Devil Dis.

However, according to all reports, the Devil is not particularly concerned about his proper name. Like the Other One, Satan takes deeds more seriously than words. Well, then, once we have identified and greeted Satan, what might we do with him?

We might organize a sabbat, particularly if it happens to be near *Walpurgisnacht* (April 30) or Allhallows Eve. Or if the local coven master doesn't want to get dressed up in all his finery, we could be content with an esbat. In the latter, one merely devotes one's time and energies to performing certain feats of magic that the local satanic community requires. The former is much more spectacular, with magic circles drawn, visiting demons conjured up, magical journeys accomplished and perhaps even a visit from Satan himself to have his bottom affectionately greeted by the members of the coven—as a prelude to intercourse with all the women present (all reports indicate that Satan is a pretty rough lover), followed by a general sexual free-for-all. The whole event is made even more ecstatic by magic potions (available from your local pusher) and frenzied dancing (rock music groups staffed by witches are available for your sabbat). In the old days, sabbats were a bit dangerous because the local officials of the Inquisition might descend upon you, but the Inquisition closed up shop some time ago, and most urban police forces have better things to do than ride herd on the Devil.

Or you might ponder the possibility of making a deal with Lucifer. The late and lamented Dr. Georg Faust (whose first name history changed to John for some inexplicable reason) is not only the most famous of the people who have traded their immortal souls to Satan for wealth, power, knowledge and pleasure. Kings, emperors and popes (most notably Sylvester II) have also been suspected of such deals, and most of the hundreds of thousands of witches executed during the witch craze of the sixteenth and seventeenth centuries confessed (under torture, of course) that they had made similar compacts with Lucifer. Dealing with Satan is a risky business, since there is substantial historical evidence that he delivers less than he promises and his broker in such matters. Mephistopheles, is something less than an honorable operative. Nonetheless, at least some of the biographers of Dr. Faust would persuade us that there exist various legal authorities who are willing to annul a contract with the Devil if one is ready to show penitence for having made such a deal. The formulas for making the contract and then getting out of it at the last minute can be found in any appropriate manual of Satanism.

There is a risk if you enter into business arrangements with the Devil that he may take possession of your soul while you are still alive. According to various reports, he frequently even takes possession of souls that have not entered into contracts with him. Under such circumstances, one always has recourse to exorcism, a practice prevalent in many pagan religions (particularly among African tribes). Exorcism has been developed to a fine art among Christians. It has been described in gripping detail in William Blatty's novel, *The Exorcist.* The Roman Church has always been reluctant to launch an exorcism and displays considerably more skepticism than many current cultists of the occult about possession. Nonetheless, the formula for exorcism, should anyone want to avail himself of it without official church auspices (and I hear this is risky) goes as follows: "I command you, ever-evil spirit, in the name of God the Father Almighty and in the name of Jesus Christ His only Son and in the name of the Holy Spirit that, harming no one, you depart from this creature of God and return to the place appointed you, there to remain forever." I'm sorry that it's not more elaborate, but the Roman Church has a disconcerting way of being simple at times when you most expect it to be baroque.

Incidentally, there is considerable debate among Roman Catholic exorcists about whether they really do encounter the Devil in such contests. Msgr. Luigi Novarase, the official exorcist of the

Diocese of Rome, is quite convinced that he has done battle with the Devil. On the other hand, Joseph de Tonquedec, who was an exocist in Paris for a half century, was convinced that he never came across a genuine case of possession. He observed, "Exorcism is an impressive ceremony, capable of acting effectively on a sick man's subconscious experience. The abjurations addressed to the demon, the sprinklings with the holy water, the stole passed around the patient's neck, the repeated signs of the cross, etc., can easily call up a diabolical mythomania in word and deed in a psyche already weak. Call the Devil and you'll see him, or rather not him, but a portrait made up of a sick man's idea of him." One Catholic author commented that the difference between Novarase and De Tonquedec may merely show that there are more devils in Rome than in Paris. But then De Tonquedec was a French Jesuit and would very properly be wary.

Sigmund Freud says much the same thing as De Tonquedec in a little-known essay, "The Neurosis of Demoniacal Possession in the Seventeenth Century," published in 1923. The Devil, according to Freud, is a father substitute for those who "never have any luck . . . [or are] too poorly gifted, too ineffective to make a living and belong to that well-known type, the eternal suckling . . . who are unable to tear themselves away from the joyous haven of the mother's breast, who hold fast all through their lives to their claim to be nourished by someone else." Several Catholic writers, re-examining the 1949 case in Washington, D.C., on which William Blatty's novel was based, are profoundly skeptical about supernatural intervention in that incident.

If you don't like exorcism, you might try a Black Mass, a ritual popular long before the Marquis de Sade recorded one variety of it in *Justine*. Since the memory of man runneth not to the contrary, an enterprising tourist with a sufficient number of francs could easily find a Black Mass in Paris. The basic elements seem to be a chalice, bread, black candles, black cloth on the table and a naked woman, preferably a virgin. Should one prove hard to locate in our permissive times, it probably wouldn't matter too much if she lacked that condition. Mass is offered with the woman's body (between the breasts) used as an altar. One may either recite the prayers of the Roman Catholic Mass backwards (as far as I know still in Latin, though there may be an English language version by now) or recite formularies parodying the Catholic words of consecration. It is also thought to be extremely helpful if you could have some consecrated Hosts stolen from a Catholic church (a practice made more difficult with the removal of the Blessed Sacrament from many Catholic altars). Ritual murders, particularly of children and babies, have apparently been practiced in Black Masses in the past. One moderately well-documented example occurred when Louis XIV's mistress, Madame de Montespan, held a Black Mass in order to get the Devil to help her hold onto the Sun King, who had begun to lose interest in her charms. (The attempt failed.) No one is likely to match the efforts of the famous marshal of France Gilles de Rais, who is alleged to have murdered between two hundred and eight hundred children in such rituals (and probably gave rise to the Bluebeard legend). Presumably, in this enlightened age, however, we can dispense with such sacrifices, though there is evidence that not all satanists are persuaded of this liturgical reform.

If rituals and compacts are relatively heavy activities, it is worth noting that the Devil hasn't always been taken that seriously. The gargoyles on the medieval cathedrals are evidence that one aspect of the medieval personality was inclined to laugh at the Devil because of its belief that the powers of evil had been beaten (a belief that from the perspective of the twentieth century looks inexcusably naïve). The medieval style of humor may not appeal to us now, but it does provide another way of dealing with the Devil. For example, St. Dunstan, Abbot of Glastonbury and later Archbishop of Canterbury, was one day busily engaged in making a Eucharist chalice when the Devil appeared to him. Quite nonchalantly, the saint look his pliers out of the fire and seized the nose of Satan, who ran off with a howl and never dared to molest that worthy again.

Finally, if Black Masses, dealing with the Devil, or tweaking his nose isn't your thing, then you could form a church of Satan and set up camp as the head of the increasing number of satanic sects in the United States. One expects that shortly these various satanic groups will begin to hold annual conventions, and not too long after that will demand one of their members be admitted to the podium in front of the Capitol building on Inauguration Day. Who knows? Maybe they have a right to be there.

Those engaged in the contemporary satanist cults frequently distinguish between white witches (those who use their power only to do good), black witches (those who use their power to harm others but are not full-fledged diabolists) and satanists (those who worship the Devil). Even satanists make a distinction between those who believe the Devil is a person and those who simply claim to be unlocking positive natural forces, somehow or other related to ESP and telekinesis. Thus a man like Anton Szandor La Vey, for all his mystical ritual (complete with sword, pentagram and fire), denies the personal reality of Satan. Indeed, many of those who are engaged in witchcraft or Satanism today will argue either that it is an ancient Celtic nature religion (and some of the advocates of this position call themselves Druids or even Archdruids) or that their craft is really scientific secular skill—perhaps even one with revolutionary, psychological or social implications. (Whether in fact contemporary witchcraft and satanist beliefs and rituals are a continuation of British Celtic nature religions is a matter of some debate. A British scholar named Margaret Murray argued sometime ago that the "Old Religion" had indeed been kept alive by a peasant underground. While there isn't much doubt that ancient superstitions survived in most European countries—and not merely in the peasant regions either—most of the doctrines and ceremonies of contemporary Satanism are a hodgepodge of Oriental and Western superstitions, owing a good deal more to Aleister Crowley, a half-mad magician and showman who tried to live up to his reputation as the Wickedest Man in the World, than to any underground survival of Druidism.

Most of contemporary native American Satanism is bunkum and hokum—as I suspect most of the earlier satanist cults were too. In time of confusion and uncertainty the unhappy, the credulous, the vaguely neurotic and those who are always seeking for some form of inside knowledge (St. Paul would have called them Gnostics) can find in Satanism a response to their emotional (and frequently to their sexual) needs. Counterculture Satanism is—like most other counterculture phenomena—partly a put-on, partly neurotic, partly an escape and partly dead serious. To the extent that it becomes dead serious, Satanism can be dangerous, as the Manson case and other ritual murders should make clear. At a minimum, it is psychologically risky to mess around with that which is professedly evil. Witches all around the world are not above using poisons to accomplish their goals, and the badly disturbed could easily be pushed into psychosis by satanist experimentation.

Finally, there are more powers under heaven that philosophy and sociology dream of (though anthropology knows them well). Whether these forces are natural or supernatural is scarcely the point. They are dangerous, and the sane, healthy person stays away from them. But is it all hokum and bunkum? Is the whole tradition of evil spirits nothing more than benighted superstition created by our ancestors, who in terms of a scientific world view were little more than howling savages?

Those who created a mythology of the Devil were trying to cope with the mystery of evil, a mystery whose existence until very recently was denied by the modern world. There was the "problem of evil," of course, which was used in sophomore philosophy classes to prove either that God didn't exist or that His existence was at best a hypothesis. But having been used for that purpose, the problem of evil was cast aside and we continued to live in our benign, scientifically ordered universe in which human evolution and technological progress could be expected to eliminate gradually all but the barest residue of evil.

Depending on whether our prophet was Freud or Marx, we explained human evil in terms of either childhood traumas or oppressive social structures. Psychoanalysis or political revolution—or perhaps even peaceful change caused by social democracy—could be expected to minimize the amount of evil in the world. Such a faith was born of the Enlightenment and came to maturity in the late nineteenth century. It began to die in Europe in 1914 and was defunct at the end of the holocaust of the Second World War. But the United States was unaffected by both wars and was for a time able to ignore the bloody religious, racial, linguistic and ethnic conflicts that have torn the world since 1945. It was only the riots, the assassinations of the sixties, and the conflicts and moral confusions of Vietnam that began to shake our faith in Enlightenment optimism, and even now that faith still flickers, as is evidenced by the attempts of the satanists to blend their doctrine with Enlightenment rationalism and evolutionary and scientific secularity.

Our primitive ancestors were under no such illusion. For them the mystery of evil was part of their everyday life. The forces of chaos and disorder threatened to sweep in, destroy their crops or herds, devastate their tiny villages and rip apart the fragile social structure of their tribes. Man was locked in battle with disorder and evil. His village, his fields, his tribe represented a precarious exercise of order against chaos. Small wonder then that the Babylonian devil, Tiamat, was symbolic of the chaos that Marduk destroyed in his act of creation. The world emerged from a battle between good and evil, order and chaos. Humankind was on the side of the ordering forces, but the evil spirits looked in from the desert or down from the hills, ready always to strike back against humankind at the slightest sign of diminished vigilance. Primitive man was conscious that he was in conflict with powers much greater than himself: disease, storm, drought, marauding tribes, conflict within his own community and the ultimate evil power of death. He had no doubt about the reality of the powers with whom he was contending, and giving these powers personalities (frequently sketchy) and names was merely a way of emphasizing the fierce battle against disorder and chaos in which he was engaged. To define them in human terms served to put inhuman forces within a more understandable and more manageable context.

The serpent in the book of Genesis represented the principle of disorder, confusion, chaos and evil in the universe. Satan contends directly against that poor suffering servant of Yahweh, Job, and tempts David to take a census. For the rest of the Old Testament Satan is not called by a proper name and seems to act as an agent of Yahweh as one of the "angels of Yahweh" (*malak Yahweh* or *bene haelohim*), that is to say, he is a manifestation of Yahweh's power not really distinct from God himself. There were demons in the Hebrew religion, but they were generally Canaanite gods who worked out in the desert.

In the New Testament, Jesus is tempted by Satan—now clearly a demon. He is cast out of people whom he has possessed; he is called "the strong one," "the evil one," "the prince of this world." Jesus' death is conceived of by some New Testament authors as a price to be paid to Satan for the liberation of humankind.

New Testament scholars debate whether frequent New Testament references to Satan are an indication that belief in a personal Devil is part of the essence of Christianity. The majority of scholars are inclined to suggest today that the New Testament writers were using the mythological and religious thought of their time to describe the titanic battle in the universe between good and evil and the Christian faith in the ultimate triumph of good. A number of Roman Catholic dogmatic theologians have rallied to Paul VI's support, while Scripture scholars have tended to remain silent. They are not at all convinced that the New Testament need be interpreted as requiring a belief in the personal reality of the Devil.

But arguing whether the Devil is a person or not may be quite beside the point, for the more appropriate issue might be whether evil is real. More specifically, have we solved the mystery of evil?

For an answer one only need pick up the newspaper or look at the TV tube: hurricanes, earthquakes, airplane crashes, railroad accidents, famines, epidemics, the destruction of the environment —physical evil is all around us. But worse is man's evil to man: tribal and ethnic wars, racial and religious bigotry, epidemics of assassination, kidnaping, skyjacking and heroin addiction; large corporation bureaucracies crumpling the dignity of human persons in the blind pursuit of power and profit. But the magnitude of the evil is not proportionate to the malice of the people involved. Many killers are men of moderate good will who intend not evil but good. The war in Vietnam—on both sides—was launched for high-minded purposes, and yet turned into a bloodbath from which neither side was able to extricate itself for years. Evil comes from mistakes, miscalculations, limitations, ignorance far more frequently than it comes from malice. If there is a superintelligence guiding the powers of evil, one must say that his strategy has been brilliant; the situation in Europe in the early 1940s, while Russia and Germany were simultaneously governed by madmen, was a stroke of incomparable evil genius. If all the disasters that afflicted the United States in the 1960s were the result of random chance, then we were extraordinarily unlucky. If one believes in personified evil, then one must say that the '60s were among his finest hours.

Freudian psychology may explain the personality of a Lee Harvey Oswald or a Sirhan Sirhan, but it cannot explain how the evil that came from their actions was so vast. Marxist or quasi-Marxist sociology may explain how imperialist countries got involved in other parts of the world, but it cannot explain why an industrial ruling class was unable for so long to end a war that it knew was in its best interest to end. Faced with the mystery of human social evil, many liberal commentators are forced to create new diabolic myths and clothe them in such phrases as "The Establishment" or "the American people." These are not really analytic categories but religious myths invented just as surely as was Tiamat or Satan to explain the immensity of the evil that goes far beyond human reason or understanding.

Our ancestors, then, were not howling savages. They were aware of an awesome reality that we tried to persuade ourselves had gone away.

Is evil personified?

As Goethe's Mephisto remarks, "I am that which cancels out. . . . Everything in existence is worthy only of destruction, so it would be better if nothing existed." Such pervasive pessimism has vigorously asserted itself in recent thought, though few are yet willing to be quite so blunt as Mephisto. Much of the romanticism, not to say irrationalism, of the counterculture (and such folk prophets as Theodore Roszak) is ultimately rooted in a yet unarticulated belief that life and existence are insane.

The question is not Black Masses or sabbats or exorcisms or the witchcraft of Anton La Vey or the fuzzy-minded Christian cleric dabbling in the occult. The question is rather whether Tiamat—Chaos—is the ultimate reality. The data are remarkably persuasive that it is.

And yet not conclusive. The forces of goodness, order, graciousness and love seem to be everywhere in retreat, on the verge of defeat, almost overwhelmed by the powers of darkness. It has always seemed that way. But humankind is incurably afflicted by the disease of hope. It may be a monstrous self-deception, the ultimate cruelty of a vicious universe; or it may be, as Peter Berger has recently argued, a "rumor of angels," a signal of the transcendent. Far more important than whether the Devil is a person is the question of whether hopefulness can be trusted. The mother in *The Exorcist* who doubted God but not the Devil echoes a nearly universal human insight. There is no reason to doubt the existence of evil in the world, but considerable uncertainty about the existence of or at least the durability of good.

So it is indeed appropriate for the principal bishop of Christianity to warn his followers and all others in the world of the existence of evil. But one wonders whether at this stage of the game there are many left who doubt it. Even in the great American universities the Enlightenment is in its death throes. It might be more appropriate for this principal bishop to remind his followers of the religious symbols that proclaim in the face of considerable evidence to the contrary that good does triumph over evil, love over hatred, life over death, comedy over tragedy. Perhaps he might reflect the vision of Dostoevski that evil is only a seedy hanger-on, or of Dante that evil is becoming more and more a victim of entropy as it sinks ever more deeply into ice, or of St. Dunstan, who tweaked the Devil in the nose with his fiery pincers and sent him off howling. Such visions of the conquest of evil or the banality of evil may be unduly naïve, but Christianity in its best moments has been committed to them.

To do that, though, might have been risky. Humankind does not object to prophets of doom, for the evidence of doom is all around. We do not grow angry when it is announced to us that the powers of darkness are making progress on all sides, for we have already noticed that the light is waning.

No, the kind of leaders we really object to are those who call us to begin over again, who tell us that the light can shine brighter and that the power of evil can be repelled. Religious and political leaders who preach a message of hope are never very welcome, for they require of us more than cynicism, more than despair, more than resignation. They require effort, activity, fidelity, commitment. The angels of light always have a hard time of it compared to the angels of darkness. If they persist in preaching their good news to us, we get rid of them; we shoot them or we crucify them. And that's the end of them.

Or is it?

CHAPTER 2

The Demon of Ressentiment and the Angel of Nobility

Max Scheler, a German social philosopher, used a French word, *ressentiment,* to title his classic study of envy. *"Ressentiment"* is not just envy; it is a systematic pathology of the little man who feels the compelling need to tear down and destroy the great man. Of all the demons that torment human life, the demon of ressentiment, of pernicious envy, is perhaps the most powerful and pervasive. Scheler tells us that it is *"existential envy,* which is directed against the other person's very *nature.* Scheler adds that ressentiment whispers continually: "I can forgive everything, but not that you *are*—that you are *what* you are—that I am not what you are—indeed that I am not *you."*[1]

It is not the other's successes or possessions or talents that are oppressive, but his very being. "This form of envy strips the opponent of his very existence, for this existence as such is felt to be a 'pressure,' a 'reproach,' and an unbearable humiliation." Scheler concludes his definition with a quotation from Goethe: "against another's great merits, there is no remedy but love."[2]

The demon of Ressentiment takes possession of the assassin, the gossip columnist, the muckraker, the investigative reporter, the small-minded politician, the second-rate scholar, the inadequate athlete, the moderately successful business and professional man. All of these people, the most of the rest of us besides, want

---

[1] Max Scheler, *Ressentiment,* edited by Lewis A. Coser, translated by William W. Holdheim. New York: Schocken Books paperback edition, 1972. Published in 1961 by The Free Press. P. 52.
[2] *Ibid.,* p. 53.

to cut others down to size. Indeed, some of the advocates of the "new egalitarianism" quite bluntly suggest that bright students be penalized so that they will have no unfair advantages over anyone else. The envious person is obsessed by greatness, fascinated by it, but deeply resents that someone else has it while he does not. "It is not fair!" says the assassin, the egalitarian, the bitter and frustrated second-rater. "It is not fair that someone else should have that which I so desperately want."

Scheler explains the psychology of ressentiment:

> Therefore such phenomena as joy, splendor, power, happiness, fortune, and strength magically attract the man of ressentiment. He cannot pass by, he has to look at them, whether he "wants" to or not. But at the same time he wants to avert his eyes, for he is tormented by the craving to possess them and knows that his desire is vain. The first result of this inner process is a characteristic *falsification* of the *world view*. Regardless of what he observes, his world has a peculiar structure of emotional stress. The more the impulse to turn away from those positive values prevails, the more he turns without transition to their negative opposites, on which he concentrates increasingly. He has an urge to scold, to depreciate, to belittle whatever he can. Thus he involuntarily "slanders" life and the world in order to justify his inner pattern of value experience.[3]

But, Scheler continues, it is not enough to falsify one's world view. In the long run it is impossible and ineffective to avert one's eyes from excellence. ". . . happiness, power, beauty, wit, goodness, and other phenomena of positive life . . . exist and impose themselves. . . . When such a quality irresistibly forces itself upon his attention, the very sight suffices to produce an impulse of hatred against its bearer, who has never harmed or insulted him."[4] And there is nothing the object of ressentiment can do about it: ". . . this hyena-like and ever-ready ferocity . . . is not caused by the 'enemy's' actions and behavior, it is deeper and more irreconcilable than any other. It is not directed against

---

[3] *Ibid.*, pp. 74–75.
[4] *Ibid.*, p. 75.

transitory attributes, but against the other person's very essence and being."[5]

The devil of ressentiment operates most clearly upon children. Few can stand the really gifted child. The young person with intelligence, ability, talent is a reproach to most of his contemporaries and not a few of his teachers. If his intellectual abilities are combined with good looks, as is frequently the case, and material wealth, then the resentment is even fiercer. Everything possible must be done to bring the deviant into line. Ridicule from both fellow students and the teachers, who may feel threatened that a child might know more than they, is commonly employed. The parents of other children are quick to encourage resentful behavior, because it is a reproach to them if someone else's child is more gifted than their own. And it is by no means infrequent for the parents of the gifted child themselves to try to reduce their offspring to a state where he is "just like everyone else." Such a punishment worked on their own flesh and blood is justified by "the child must learn to fit in"; "he mustn't get a big head"; and "he might get into trouble later on if he takes himself too seriously." A report card with solid A's is scarcely noticed, but if a B happens to appear, then that is what is commented on. Other children who seem to be less gifted must be protected, the parents tell us, from the trauma of having to compete with the gifted one. Nothing is said, of course, about what happens to a young person who is penalized for his own excellence.

Almost all of this parental justification for punishing the gifted child is pretense; indeed, some of it is hypocrisy. For parents are threatened by a bright child just like everyone else. They want to see him cut down to size, at least as much as his classmates.

Unfortunately the young victim of envy has no experience that will enable him to understand what is happening. He alone does not experience envy; he has no particular need to, and very likely admires and respects other talent rather than being threatened by it. One cannot understand or respond to a human emotion

[5] *Ibid.*

which one has not experienced oneself. The child who is the victim of envy simply does not understand why so many people dislike him. He works hard, he attempts to be generous and friendly to others, and yet for some reason that completely escapes him, they seem bent on doing mean, vicious, nasty things to him.

The force of ressentiment usually works with children. Most are brought into line; they continue to do well, of course, but they moderate their talents, they limit their abilities, they restrict their productivity. They will not be "ratebusters"; it is much better, the child argues, not to do all the things one likes to do if the cost of being good at everything is to be disliked, punished, and resented by one's friends, teachers, brothers and sisters, and even parents. Heaven only knows how much talent, how much genius has been lost to the human race because of the terrible price some gifted children have had to pay. I worked for a long time as a parish priest in a community where for a number of strange reasons what may well have been the last flowering of Irish-American literary greatness showed signs of taking place. The community was a kind of Listowel, located not in County Kerry but County Cook.[6] But virtually none of the young people who grew up in that neighborhood ever set a serious word down on paper. The costs were simply too high; the resentment from their family and their friends over their abilities was too powerful for them to even begin to think about developing abilities that they knew they had. It was a tragic, senseless waste, a waste caused by envy that was neither unconscious nor undeliberate.

The envious person can always count on social support. The community will quickly agree that whatever he says about the gifted person, no matter how false or outrageous or absurd, is true. The object of envy may periodically feel that he is losing his mind, for everyone around him seems to agree with charges

---

[6] Listowel is a small market town in the west of Ireland which, for reasons no one fully understands, has produced an incredible number of writers. As one native put it to me, "In the last half century we have produced six playwrights, five poets, four novelists, and you have to fight your way through the essayists as you go down the street."

and accusations that he knows are absurd. Yet rarely, if ever, will the community break ranks. The conspiracy of silence which supports the envious person must be maintained; envy is too important a mechanism of social control to be endangered. The envious persons, the Iagos of the world, may be vicious, nasty sneaks, but no one ever assassinates them; and rarely if ever will anyone tell them to their faces that they are phonies and frauds. To put the matter more concretely, no one ever tells us to put aside the devil ressentiment when he threatens to dominate our personality.

Envy is a deadly poison when it gets into our bloodstreams. It infects everything we do and say. The desire to cut down those who seem to be better than we are takes such possession of us that we have little time or energy left for anything else. The Lee Harvey Oswalds and the Sirhan Sirhans—both classic examples of the ambivalence, the love-hate, that marks ressentiment—were only caricatures of the demon of Envy that operates in each one of us. Goodness, excellence, beauty, greatness are intolerable; they must not be permitted to persist in the world.

Envy gets much more sophisticated and subtle in adult life. The business corporation, the university, the mass media, the professional guild all have room for talented people so long as they are not too talented or too gifted. What usually happens is a compromise: the talented novice learns to be properly diffident and discreet. He performs well but not too well; he learns how to fit in, how not to threaten his seniors or unduly disturb his peers. He gets ahead, but he restrains himself so that he does not move ahead too quickly. Normally this process need not be conscious or explicit. The adult has learned long ago that, to make it in the world, one must be good but not too good, gifted but not too gifted, able but not too able. Some people, of course, never learn. They prove quite incapable of discovering the fine line between acceptable achievement and overachievement. If they are really gifted and lucky, they may make it anyhow. They may eventually stop caring about whether people like them or not and become quite content with lives of lonely eminence. Still they would do well to reflect on what Mozart's rivals did to him. He died in lonely, desperate circumstances, an outcast from his world of music and written off as a failure. Mozart was an overachiever. He wrote too much; there was simply no room for him in the Vienna of his day. But is there room for such genius in any city at any time?

In this chapter I have described the ressentiment that the small feel for the great, the petty feel for the magnificent, the ugly feel for the beautiful, the second-rate feel for the first-rate, the ordinary feel for the genius. But of course most of the operations of the demon of envy are not directed at the Mozarts of this world. There are too few of them to keep the demon of Ressentiment occupied for much of the time. Most of the envy generated in the human race is aimed at those who are only a little better than we are—the priest who preaches sermons that are slightly better than ours, the teacher who has somewhat more success with students than we do, the woman down the street who seems to be somewhat more sexy than we are, the family next door who seems to have more money than we do, the kid across the aisle whose grade-point average is slightly higher than ours, the quarterback whose completion average is four or five percentage points above our own. Ressentiment is broad-minded; he doesn't discriminate, he persecutes the great, the near-great, and those who are just a little bit better with equal enthusiasm and vigor. He may be small, nasty, sneaky, and vicious this Demon of Envy, but he makes up for these deficiencies by his tireless efforts, boundless resourcefulness, energy, and impassioned dedication to his goals. Only when the human race has become completely bland and banal, only when no one ever dares to step out of line, only when the last vestige of ingenuity and creativity is eliminated from the race will there be no work left for the Demon of Envy to do.

Why?

Why are most of us pushovers for this unattractive but persistent demon? Why is envy the third most powerful motivation affecting humankind? (After self-preservation and sex.) Why do we all conspire to avoid mentioning its existence? Why, for all its power, is it such a secret vice? There is no fun or enjoyment, no laughter or good times, no refreshment or entertainment in envy. He is a grim, deadly serious, utterly debilitating demon. Why then is he so important to us?

The answer is easy enough. Someone else's excellence (even if it is only slightly above our own) is seen as a reflection on our lack of excellence. If he is good, we are no good; if he is beautiful, we are ugly; if he is smart, we are dumb; if he is rich, we are poor; if he is quick, we are slow; if he is popular, we are outcast. It is not fair that he should be so attractive. The envious person will not accept himself as he is, but insists that he be someone else.

The ultimate root of envy is our inability to accept ourselves for who and what we are. If we could believe the measure of our own goodness is what we do with what we have, then there would be no need for envy. But if the measure of our own goodness is a comparison of ourselves with other people, then envy is inevitable. If goodness is based on some absolute standard, then indeed it is not fair that abilities, talents and good looks are unequally distributed. But if goodness is based on a standard which asks what we have done with what we have, then the unequal distribution of gifts is not unjust. The standard of comparison will then be, what am I capable of being? Envy becomes senseless in that perspective. But the angel who comes to whisper that comparison with others is foolish has his work cut out for him. Most of us are trained from early years to compare ourselves unfavorably with others human beings instead of with our own capacities. Scheler, commenting on the work of Georg Simmel, notes that comparison is built into the human condition, but there are different kinds of comparisons:

> The noble man's naive self-confidence, which is as natural to him as tension is to the muscles, permits him calmly to assimilate the merits of others in all the fullness of their substance and configuration. He never "grudges" them their merits. On the contrary: he rejoices in their virtues and feels that they

make the world more worthy of love. His naive self-confidence is by no means "compounded" of a series of positive valuations based on specific qualities, talents, and virtues: it is originally directed at his very *essence* and *being*. Therefore he can afford to admit that another person has certain "qualities" superior to his own or is more "gifted" in some respects—indeed in all respects. Such a conclusion does not diminish his naive awareness of his own value, which needs no justification or proof by achievements or abilities. Achievements merely serve to confirm it.[7]

The "common" man, according to Scheler, "can only experience his value and that of another if he relates the two and he clearly perceives" the differences.[8] He is valuable only if he compares "favorably" with the other. As Scheler puts it, "The noble man experiences value *prior to* any comparison, the common man *in* and *through* a comparison."[9] The angel of light, therefore, must insist that we have basic and fundamental value without any need of comparing ourselves to others. Such an angel of light, who might be appropriately named the Angel of Nobility, has not a particularly successful record thus far in the history of humankind. One needs intense confidence in the goodness of the universe to believe that it is really all right to accept oneself as one is, with inherent dignity, nobility and worth quite independent of any comparison with others.

One of the most nasty aspects of the Demon of Ressentiment is his capacity to take on the guise of piety. Some of the most vicious acts of envy masquerade as exercises in high virtue.

I would be hard put not to say that envy is worse in the Church than it is in the university world. I do not think that the secular university is so passionately eager to destroy its own great. A brilliantly gifted loyal churchman like Hans Küng would not be submitted to the constant envious assaults he must endure in the Church if he were associated with a secular university. On the

[7] Scheler, *op. cit.*, pp. 54–55.
[8] *Ibid.*, p. 55.
[9] *Ibid.*, p. 55.

other hand, academic envy, while not as passionate as ecclesiastical envy, tends to be more petty. There is in the professorate, I think, more nasty senseless infighting than there is in the clergy. The comparison should be a foolish one; the religious commitment of priests ought to lead them to much more generous and open conduct than could possibly be expected from professors. Oddly enough, it is the religious communities that are most explicitly committed to providing support and encouragement for their members who frequently are the most effective at cutting everyone down to the same size and mediocrity. The American Jesuits seem really to have discovered John Murray and Gustave Weigel only after these great men were dead. The Angel of Nobility is not much more successful among committed Christians, even among committed Christian leaders, than he (or she) is anywhere else. When dealing with religious people the Angel of Nobility must also contend with envy masquerading as piety.

Ressentiment makes our lives mean, narrow, and shabby; it sucks joy, beauty, goodness, and generosity out of our experience. We cannot permit ourselves to bask in the light of excellence, beauty, and goodness because we are incapable of enjoying such qualities for what they are. We must get out the scales and begin measuring ourselves against what we are witnessing. The devil of ressentiment does indeed protect us from feeling worthless, or at least from having to cope with our feelings of worthlessness; but he does so only after exacting a high price: he takes all the fun out of our lives. Even when we know what he is up to, we still let him get away with it.

The Angel of Nobility, on the other hand, really demands very little of us. All he asks is that we be generous. If we can say to hell with comparisons, he will promise a life that is free to enjoy beauty, goodness, excellence, and greatness whenever we encounter it. The Angel of Nobility leads us to shout "hosanna" whenever we encounter excellence. The Demon of Ressentiment urges us to cry, "Crucify him!"

Alas, there are not many hosannas ringing out now.

CHAPTER 3

The Demon of Alienation and
the Angel of Loyalty

We are all born trapped. We are constrained by the limitations of time and space, physical and cultural, which characterize the environment that surrounds us when we come into the world. Try as we might we cannot experience what it was like to be a medieval knight or a twenty-first-century space pilot. Man cannot experience what it is like to be a woman; a white cannot experience blackness; someone who has never been in military combat cannot know what combat is like.[1] We come into the world with considerable baggage of language, culture, religion, social class, and ethnic group; and we rapidly acquire further baggage of childhood and adolescent experience. I am not a Navajo Indian, and though they may admit me as a blood brother, I never will be a Navajo. Similarly, a Navajo may become a precinct captain on the south side of Chicago, but that doesn't make him Irish. We are not, of course, completely predetermined by our genetic inheritance, our environment, our early family experiences. We can transcend at least some of the limits that biology, culture,

[1] It is irrelevant to the theme of this book, but lest I be misunderstood, let me note here that while we cannot experience what others have—indeed we can experience no one else's experience but our own—sensitivity, imagination, and creativity can enable us to understand another's experience.

A woman novelist, for example, may understand much better than any man the dilemmas facing contemporary man. Her experiences of his dilemmas may be vicarious, but she may still understand them better than a man. We do not have to *be* someone else in order to *understand* them. However, some intellectual romantics would persuade us that the experiences of certain classes of people are closed book to those who do not belong to that class. Such an argument is rubbish.

and psychology impose on us, but we can break out of those limitations of time and space only with great difficulty. Frequently such breakings with our heritages involve turmoil and pain. There is much of our physical, social, and psychological heritage about which we can do nothing. We are born with many of our demons and collect most of the others in the early years of life. From one point of view original sin is nothing more than the collection of demons that we all must fight to achieve mature, responsible adulthood.

But if all our devils come from our genetic, cultural, and psychological heritages, so do all our angels. There are many things wrong, God knows, with being Irish Catholic in Chicago, and many of my own problems are tied up with that heritage. On the other hand, many of the good things about me are also clearly attributable to that heritage. I have little choice about either. My heritage, like all heritages, is a mixture of light and dark, good and bad, asset and liability. I am not predetermined to good or evil, creativity or stagnation by where I came from, but I am kidding myself if I think that where I came from isn't with me wherever I go. I can maximize the assets and minimize the liabilities, but those liabilities are still there, inextricably linked with the assets.

A psychologist once remarked to me (not apropo of myself, incidentally) that she knew a priest who was beginning to make progress when he stopped blaming the seminary for his problems. He was making really substantial progress when he stopped blaming his family; and he was close to health when he could distinguish the good from the bad, destructive from constructive in both his seminary and family experiences. Such health, unfortunately, is hard to achieve for priests and for everyone else too.

Like it or not we stand on the shoulders of those who came before us. We are painfully in debt to them for our language, our knowledge, our wisdom, our science, our technology, our religion, our ethics, and our moral sensitivity—for virtually everything we have and are. Even our capacity to judge the weakness and the limitations, the frailties and the failures of our predecessors is based on the moral perspectives and the value systems they have handed down to us. Our efforts to liberate ourselves from the constraints of the past—of course, we all must make such efforts— are nonetheless validated in the terms that the past has provided for us. We judge what has gone before us by the values of those who preceded us, for there is no place else we can acquire values. We may indeed improve somewhat those values, or, more likely, we improve our sensitivity in applying them. Still we wouldn't have the values to improve upon unless others had fashioned them throughout the many centuries before us.

The Demon of Alienation comes along and whispers in our ear that we can only be free, we can only be fully and authentically ourselves when we can break decisively and completely with our heritage. "Get out," he insists, "or they will destroy you just like they destroy everyone else." Of course he never bothers to tell us that the "they" we are trying to escape have already been internalized and become a permanent part of our personality.

The alienation myth has been a central theme of Western culture for several centuries. In other times, in other places, the Alienation Demon was properly assigned to a different kind of work. In most of the environments humankind has known breaking decisively with one's heritage was inconceivable. One can only be alienated (short of total mental collapse) when there is someplace else to go. But with the rise of the industrial metropolis and the collapse of the old peasant and feudal societies, alienation has become an option and, for some people, a necessity. One can leave one's place behind, be it a native country, a home town, a neighborhood, an ethnic community, or a belief system.

The option of departing has been converted into a symbol of growth and freedom. The great poet, the great artist, the great thinker, the great political leader are presented to us as having gone through the agony of "breaking" with their heritages and thereby becoming free to be "themselves." There is no doubt that the great painters of the nineteenth century flocked from the countryside to Paris, and most American writers leave the plains, the hills, the hinterlands behind to go to Boston, New York, San Francisco. Most of those in the arts who have achieved eminence in the last century have indeed left behind not only their physical environment but most of their friends and families and many of the values that constituted their social and cultural environments. Alienation has been the price that many at least have had to pay for creativity. (Not all, of course. Flannery O'Connor, J. F. Powers, William Faulkner stayed home.) But if alienation is the price some people have to pay, it does not follow that when we are alienated we will become creative. On the contrary, for most of us alienation only produces loneliness, confusion, and isolation.

If one reads the biographies of such Protestant intellectuals as Robert Bellah, Harvey Cox, and Sam Keane; such Catholics as James T. Farrell and John O'Hara; such Jewish writers are Philip Roth and Norman Podhoretz (at least the Podhoretz of *Making It*, if not the current one), one soon discovers how profound and painful has been the experience of alienation. Cox, alone of those I have mentioned, seems able to go beyond nostalgia in recollecting where he came from. The others, and hundreds like them, are still angry. They are angry at the environment which constrained them, angry, perhaps, at themselves for the deep feelings of ambivalence and guilt they have about what they have left behind.

And there may be pain and a sense of loss, but this aspect of the alienation experience of the intellectual rarely makes it into print. Some of my friends admit in unguarded moments (or mildly inebriated ones) that they miss what has been left behind. One friend in particular goes into deep depressions every Christmas when he remembers the joys of Christmas past, joys which he feels he can never recapture. (I am not so sure that he can't recapture them, but the cost he would have to pay in terms of self-awareness would be great. So would be the payoffs.)

The alienation myth may have been valid in the past (though I suspect that it was always a romantic exaggeration), but surely in the present time of high fidelity records, television, RFD, and the jet airplane there is enough physical, intellectual, and psychological mobility so that no one needs to claim that he is trapped by his environment. The myth of the alienated intellectual in contemporary circumstances is a self-fulfilling prophecy. The intellectual becomes alienated because he is persuaded that unless he is alienated he won't be considered intellectual. A lot of would-be, quasi- and pseudo-intellectuals feel they must go through the posture and pretense of alienation to acquire a cosmopolitan veneer. Graduate schools, professional schools, and the institutions that train artists, musicians, and actors, as well as the colleges that feed their graduates into the elite universities, all assume that it is necessary to deracinate the young person as a prelude to making him an intellectual. Hence, training in the quality colleges and universities assumes that alienation is desirable. Authenticity, integrity, autonomy, liberation all demand that one be free from the biases, the perspectives, the values of one's neighborhood, one's town, one's social class, one's church. College and graduate school are for many young people merely a rite of passage from one ethnic community to another. Changed they are, but liberated, hardly.

I have always been amused by the comments of some young political activists who discover while they are canvassing the precincts that voters are not stereotypical bigots but complex, interesting, and, on the whole, not unintelligent human beings. Such young people are in fact rediscovering their families and finding out that they are not nearly so bad as their professors had claimed.

To a considerable extent the McGovern movement was an attempt on the part of the self-alienated cultural elites to take control of the country. The movement failed because the McGovern elite simply did not understand that middle America for which it felt so much contempt. The irony, of course, is that most of the McGovern enthusiasts were themselves products of middle America. What they did not understand and could not communicate with was that population group from which they had come.

One would have thought that the failure of the new political

class to win power with McGovern would have led to a recon-
sideration of whether alienation is necessary as a prerequisite to
freedom and creativity, but those who are flocking to the counterculture maintain that freedom consists of breaking the bonds of
heritage. Unfortunately they often assume the stronger constrain-
ing bonds of the commune, whose rigidities are at least as inflexible as those of the ethnic neighborhood or small town. The
young people may think they are liberated, but they have ex-
changed one form of slavery for another.

The Alienation Demon is a liar. He says, "You gotta leave
home." Then, once you have left, he says, "You can't go home
again." It may well be true that psychologically and economically
one must leave behind the physical place in which one grew up.
It may also be psychologically and physically impossible to return
to it; but the alienation devil is kidding us and we are kidding
ourselves when we think that we do not carry "home" with us.
The alienated Irish Catholic is still an Irish Catholic to the core
of his being even if he stops going to church and ridicules
everything Irish. The alienated Jew is still a Jew even if he
changes his name and breaks the dietary laws every time he sits
down at the table. The fundamentalist Protestant is still a rigid
moral enthusiast even when he has become an agnostic full professor at an elite university. (Harvey Cox has the good sense to
realize that he is still very much an American Baptist.) We bring
our heritages with us; all alienation does is to make us think that
they have been left behind. They are with us still, but that they
are silent partners does not make them any less important or influential.

For a decade I lived in the University of Chicago community.
It was an exciting, interesting place. Brilliant, articulate people
abounded, there was a vigorous cultural life, fascinating cocktail
parties and dinners, and a brisk, challenging atmosphere with
never a dull moment. I used to joke that Hyde Park was a
neighborhood just like any other neighborhood in the city with
the only difference being that it was more integrated (well, at
least blacks and whites lived in physical juxtaposition) and better

educated. But after a while I discovered that Hyde Park was not like other neighborhóods. Most of the people in it had gone through the alienation experience; they had no turf of their own, no ground on which to stand, no roots, personal or religious or social. They lived in Hyde Park as temporary residents (even if they had been there for thirty years). They were committed to their careers, certain universalistic values, and also to mutual self-defense against crime; but they were for the most part people who had left home and were convinced they could never go home again. Hyde Park was at best a counterfeit home.[2] Many such people enthusiastically quote Herbert Marcuse's *One Dimensional Man* without realizing that there is a dimension of depth missing from their own lives, depth that can only come from having a ground of your own and a set of ultimate values to which you are deeply committed. Along with Marx they may rage at the alienation of the contemporary industrial masses. In fact, however, most of the masses do have a place of their own; they are not nearly as alienated as the intellectuals think they are or as the intellectuals themselves in fact are.

The damage that a neighborhood like Hyde Park does is particularly evident in its children. Part of growing up is to fight one's parents' values. Such a conflict undoubtedly means some kind of temporary estrangement from one's own place, one's own social and intellectual turf. An interlude of alienation is part of the maturation experience in our mobile, flexible society. The trouble with our intellectual elite is that they remain fixed in that developmental level. The problem for their children is that there is nothing to rebel against, nothing to be temporarily estranged from. If the parents have no values other than the vague universalistic principles of academic liberalism, then what value

[2] There are some university faculty and community residents for whom Hyde Park is quite literally home. They were born and raised in the community and never left there. The university's distinguished president, Edward Levi, is one of these. Such second-, third-, and quite possibly fourth-generation Hyde Park intellectuals are anything but alienated. They have been able to eat their cake and have it too, to be intellectual and to belong to a neighborhood.

systems do you rub against as you struggle to develop a value system of your own? If your parents don't live "anywhere," how in the hell can you go away from the place where they are? Not all Hyde Park children, not even large numbers of them, are psychological misfits; indeed, a considerable number of Hyde Park intellectuals are not nearly as alienated as they think. Nevertheless, given the psychological sophistication about child-rearing that exists in Hyde Park, there are many disturbed children. The parents have done all the right things according to the most advanced and best research in the literature. But since many of them do not believe in anything, there are no values for their children to absorb, fight against, and then integrate into their personalities. First-generation alienation—when it is more than just a passing developmental phase—is a painful, isolating experience; second-generation alienation, particularly in an intellectual environment that displays little belief in anything anymore, frequently produces total personality disorientation.

If one could see anomie as one can see the muddy waters of a flood when it courses through a town, the streets of Hyde Park would be waist deep in the stuff. Sometimes I think that it has already risen to the first floor of the houses.

I finally got the hell out of Hyde Park, not because I didn't like the people—I do—but because the rootlessness and the moral anomie of the place (even though most of the people in it are, out of habit if nothing else, highly moral individuals) was just too much to live with. In a choice between a neighborhood where the value system is too tight and one where there isn't any value system (though much pontification about values), I would pick the former. I hope (and believe) that there are other options available.

The real question, then, is not whether you can leave home— you can't, home comes with you—the question is rather whether you can be explicit about home, whether you can understand it, accept it. It is at this point that the Angel of Loyalty appears on the scene. This worthy spirit does not seek for unquestioning loyalty, for such loyalty is just the other side of the alienation coin (a proposition I will discuss later). The Angel of Loyalty is not a blind, stubborn, inflexible spirit. On the contrary, he is a critical spirit, requiring of us good, long, hard looks at our heritages. But that look is not the investigation made by a lawyer preparing a case for trial. Home should be subjected to searching, penetrating, critical evaluation. But unlike justice the Angel of Loyalty does not demand that the scales be balanced blindfolded. "Take a good hard look at home," says this evenhanded spirit. "Let there be no doubt in your mind that it may be narrow, inflexible, repressive; but also be clear that it offered goodness, richness, warmth, and support." Only if you can combine sympathy with criticism will you ever be able to deal with home as a mature adult. Since home is you, you will only be able to accept and understand yourself when you can respond to it both critically and sympathetically.

It is both bad and good to be Irish Catholic (or a Jew, or a Pole, or a Texan, or whatever else you might be). You may be able to transcend some of the bad, you may—though heaven forgive you—repress some of the good, but if you wish to understand your assets and liabilities you should approach your heritage with an open mind. If you are ashamed of it then you are ashamed of yourself, and that is precisely what the Demon of Alienation has in mind when he designs his field of torment.

I characterize alienation in ethnic categories, because such categories are so important to American society and because I earn my living just now by studying ethnic groups. One could just as well substitute other categories, particularly personality styles. We cannot shed our own personalities and acquire others just as we cannot shed an ethnic heritage or acquire another. We can develop and enrich our own, but not even the most expensive psychotherapy or analysis can fashion a totally new style personality for us to don as we would a new dress or new suit.

It is difficult to maintain a balance, to respect and admire one's family, friends, one's religious, ethnic, and geographic heritage

while still being keenly aware of the limitations of that heritage
and how those limitations limit us because we are part of it. It is
difficult to respect that which we are and still strive to transcend
it. Like all the other angels, the Angel of Loyalty has a more complex argument to make than the demon of alienation. He says,
"Get out!" The angel says, "Leave, but stay too." The demon
says, "You can't go home again." The angel says, "You can go
home again if you want to."

Alienation can become cosmic. It is now fashionable to hate
not only one's own immediate cultural heritage but the entire
republic of which we are a part. America, we are told repeatedly,
is a sick society, and the American people are a sick people.
Exactly what such global condemnation means is difficult to tell
when no one seems to be able to offer an example of a "healthy"
society and people. Occasionally they may mention Sweden or
Holland, but if you can offer personal experience of those countries, that argument fades quickly. The Demon of Alienation
thrives on sweeping condemnation. There is no room for nuance,
no room to distinguish between successes and failures, between
ideals and their achievement, between principle and practice,
between perfection and honest effort. Out goes the bath water,
and no matter that there might be a baby in it.

Similarly, during the 1960s, in the wave of fluidity and excitement that swept American Catholicism after the Vatican Council,
virtually everything that had been done before 1960 was jetti-
soned. Celibacy, the parochial schools, the religious life, most of
our critical religious symbols, reverence, the sacred—all had to go
down the drain. They were part of the Tridentine church or
immigrant Catholicism, and nothing that was Tridentine or immigrant could possibly be any good. Enthusiasts (mostly priests
and religious) soon found that, having alienated themselves from
everything, they had nothing left to believe in, no ground on
which to stand. Having proclaimed that ecumenism meant that
there were no longer any important religious differences, they
were incapable of finding any special or unique contributions that

Catholicism of Christianity had to make. The lives of many had been propped up by external restraints; when those restraints were removed, their lives collapsed. Others panicked and tried desperately to recapture the whole past, complete with rosary devotions, the Sorrowful Mother Novena, and benediction of the Blessed Sacrament.[3] The Angel of Loyalty must be close to despair. First, respect for where we came from was banished in the name of comprehensive criticism; now criticism is forgotten so that one can find some sort of security by recapturing not the substance of the past but its paraphernalia. Somehow we seemed to have passed through sympathetic and respectful criticism for about five minutes going up and about thirty seconds coming down.

Yet, of course, all of us are products of Tridentine immigrant Catholicism. The dramatic change to the new Church may have hit us at different ages of adult life, but at whatever age, the impact of change has demanded dramatic readjustments. To reject completely the pre-Vatican II Church is to reject ourselves. The younger generation of Catholic scholars, like my friend John Shea, are able to be very sympathetic and respectful now toward institutions like the immigrant parish and even to its tough presiding monsignor. They do not want or expect to go back to that parish, and they certainly would not want to work in it (and probably would not work for an old-fashioned monsignor, if one could still be found). Still they know how much they owe to the immigrant parishes and the hardfisted men who held them together. The more people who appreciate the past, the more easier breathes the Angel of Loyalty (if angels breathe).

There is a paradox here, and it will recur frequently in this book: the demon has on his side simplicity, fear, and self-rejection; the angel has on his side complexity, balance, and self-possession. The angel, then, is clearly at a disadvantage. Still, the

[3] I do not intend to criticize any of these devotions. I am suggesting that for not a few of my colleagues the desperate return to these devotional forms—and the search for religious experience in Pentecostalism—is a frantic attempt to go home again without being quite sure where home is.

self-possessed man, who knows where he came from, where he stands, and what his turf is and who can go beyond that turf, is far more attractive than the alienated, isolated critic who rants about everything that has made him what he is. Such a critic only reveals how little he thinks of himself.

CHAPTER 4

The Gnostic Demon and the Angel of Wisdom

The Alienation Demon is a new model, but the Gnostic Demon is as old as humankind. He has changed his style now and has found himself to be much busier. The old gnosticisms used to last for centuries. The Demon could sit back and enjoy watching them at work, but the new gnosticisms change yearly and sometimes even monthly. The Gnostic Demon must be almost as agile on his feet as those who are trapped in the endless struggle to be "with it."

Like the Demon of Alienation the Gnostic Demon appeals to fundamental human experience. We are afraid that we are trapped by our cultural and familial backgrounds, and the Alienation Demon says, "Get out," forgetting to tell us that we can't. Similarly we are afraid of how little we know about how to live. Even when the scientific enlightenment was riding high most of us were not scientists. The knowledge we acquired from science was derived knowledge, revealed knowledge; and although we were told that the process of revelation was different from that of the old revelation, we still looked to science for the secrets of the universe that would enable us to live richer and better lives. The Gnostic Demon takes advantage of that quest. He whispers in our ear, "See, I've got a secret, and it's the Real Secret. If you know it you will be superior to everyone else." The gnostic temptation appeals to our desire to achieve superiority over other human beings through secret knowledge they lack.

Secret societies of one sort or another have been around for a long time. Primitive tribes have them, gnostic cults rivaled early

Christianity, medieval society was honeycombed by secret fraternities, and the Masons and similar groups, at one time at least, represented the gnosticism of the Enlightenment.

What is new about contemporary gnosticism is that the secrets change so fast. There is nothing more trite than yesterday's secrets, nothing more out of date than last year's new wisdom. Our secret-hungry, wisdom-lusting industrial society gobbles up new revelations at a prodigious rate. Fashions change, and modern gnosticisms move quickly from being perennial wisdom to last month's fad.

One would have thought on a priori grounds, and many philosophers bravely predicted in the first part of this century, that it would be the "masses" who would be most prone to faddism. Their "alienation" in the "anomic," "soulless" industrial city, their lack of intellectual sophistication, their constant exposure to the degrading popular culture of the mass media—all would make them sitting ducks to the lastest exploitive fad.

But the philosophers who lamented the appearance of the "deracinated masses" were wasting their tears. Urban society divided itself up into neighborhoods, many of which became reconstructed peasant villages. They may have been narrow, provincial places, they may even have been places where fads like hula hoops spread without resistance; but the ethnic neighborhoods were powerfully resistant to the influence of the fashionable gnosticisms. The intellectual descendants of the philosophers who damned the urban masses for being rootless and soulless now damned them for being "reactionary" and "parochial."

Oddly enough, it is precisely the better educated elements in the population who are the most likely to succumb to the gnostic temptation. There are, I think, two reasons for this phenomenon. First of all, the better educated are simply more likely to read, and so they are more likely to be in contact with those journals whose responsibility it is to disseminate the latest fashions, fads, myths, and gnoses. All one need do is to subscribe to five or six magazines and newspapers (*The New York Review of Books*, the *Village Voice*, the *Partisan Review*, *The New Yorker*, *The*

Christian Century, and the *Commonweal* will do). Then one can reasonably expect to be informed about what is if not the absolutely latest revelation at least the one of a month ago. Indeed, one can keep up on the latest fads without ever having to go to New York. If one wishes to know about the new revelations before they get into the journals, then one must go to New York to become part of one of its many competing mystery cults. This is a very hard life, and not recommended for the faint of heart.

Secondly, most of those who are educated are in fact only half educated. They may be very good at what they were trained to do for a living. They have learned to be articulate and can talk persuasively about anything whether they know much about it or not. Furthermore, knowing a lot about what they do is scarcely likely to predispose them to humility about anything else. Professor Noam Chomsky, a genius in linguistics, subjects himself to little self-questioning in his pontifications on foreign policy. Indeed it is the mark of many well-educated Americans that they lack self-doubt on every subject. To be uncertain, hesitant, to admit that one does not know all the answers is to lose face somehow, to be a failure as an intellectual. Here is where the Gnostic Demon has a field day. It is impossible to know everything about everything. An article, a luncheon meeting, a brief conversation cannot serve as the basis for broad and sweeping generalizations. When it becomes an obligation to have an articulate opinion on everything, the Gnostic Demon is only too happy to provide one.

There are all kinds of fads. The McGovern movement with its sublime self-confidence and its abysmal political ignorance was one of the great gnostic interludes of our time. The Cold War certainly took on the rigidity of unquestioned secret wisdom, and so has the more recent neoisolationism, which finds the New York *Times* sounding like the Chicago *Tribune* of the 1930s. The cult of the black militants and of the self-professed lesbians who speak for only tiny proportions of their self-proclaimed constituencies is sheer gnosticism. Picketing and confrontation, name-calling and even violence continued to be popular as ordinary political tactics long after it was clear they were no longer politically effective.

There are intellectual fashions. Every academic discipline is wracked by them, and the more unstable and uncertain the discipline the more frequent the fads. (In the time since I became a sociologist my own particular research tradition, the national sample survey, has been in and out of fashion at least three times. That I am not sure whether it is fashionable at this moment or not is probably attributable to my not caring anymore.)

Ideas abound about whether American society is "healthy" or "sick," whether industrial society is "good" or "bad," whether ideology has come to an end or is being reborn, whether we are going through a period of secularization or resacralization, whether integration or segregation is socially desirable, whether ethnicity is a good or a bad thing for American society.[1]

There are life-style fads—marijuana, human potential, open marriage, long hair, the elimination of bras and girdles, natural food, foreign cars, ecology, recycling, *The Whole Earth Catalog*— one could go on and on. Not all of these new interests and concerns are necessarily false or phony. On the contrary, there may be much that is good and true in them. The gnostic may not have acquired a false secret; he has part of the truth and he thinks it

---

[1] I digress here to proclaim a special interest in this particular gnosticism, since I earn my living out of the resurgence of interest in ethnicity. This resurgence, of course, is pure fad. Ethnicity was always there; we never doubted it out in the neighborhoods. The resurgence is in fact the rediscovery of ethnicity by a few worthy journalists who have noted its existence in Manhattan (Jimmy Breslin would say Queens). These journalists have recently announced that ethnicity is over now, and if enough members of the Cambridge-Berkeley-Manhattan-Chevy Chase elite repeat this often enough, ethnicity will indeed go out of business, which is to say that my colleagues and I will seek other means of earning our livings. Note well that the rise and possible fall of the ethnicity fad will occur quite independently of whether we have come to understand anything more about ethnic diversity. My own guess is that interest in ethnicity may just be powerful enough to withstand the death notices which have appeared in some of the elite journals.

is the whole truth. To put the matter more precisely, the gnostic is the man who knows a little bit about part of the truth and thinks he knows everything. There is about many gnostics, a trace of paranoia. It is not merely that he has acquired some secret—the health-giving potential of wheat germ and pure yogurt, let us say—it is the secret they have known all along and have been hiding. "They" may take it away from "us" unless we vigorously resist them, and "we," as the bearers of truth, must preach it to the ignorant and benighted masses.

The old gnostics were not above making converts, but they were not manic proselytizers. The new gnostics—perhaps under the influence of a couple of thousand years of Christian history—are enthusiasts who have to have converts. Listen to a gnostic at a cocktail party preaching the latest secret, which he may have picked up earlier in the day in a conversation at lunch. The new knowledge is delivered with a passion, a conviction, sincerity and articulateness that would do credit to the apostle Paul if he should show up at the same party. The gnostic's voice is angry, facial muscles are drawn, the cocktail glass clutched tightly. Here is truth, pure and simple and undivided. One fails to listen at the risk of remaining ignorant and failing to achieve the moral superiority of the enlightened.

It is an arduous task to keep up. One mustn't lag behind the avant-garde. Keeping one's antennae up all the time in order to keep at least a half step ahead of the thundering masses is difficult indeed. Jewish journalists and Protestant theologians seem to be the most skilled in the art of twisting and turning so as to miss nary a signal. Catholics are much less skillful, perhaps because they only recently acquired antennae.[2]

[2] Suppose one had to choose between those two splendid trend-measuring newsletters produced by the Thomas More Association, *Context,* written by Martin Marty, and *Overview,* originally written by Dan Herr, now by Mike McCauley. *Overview* is funny, sardonic, and more unpredictable than *Context,* which is surely in much better tune with the trends. The difference between Marty and other trend-measuring Protestant theologians is that, as a good social historian, he merely notes the trends. Others seem compelled to live them.

One of the most poignant examples of the success of the Gnostic Demon was the cult of the Catholic radical in the late '60s and early '70s. An immense amount of newspaper copy and television time was taken up by this small handful of the Catholic population. Books were dedicated to the brothers Berrigan. Their books appeared in all the bookstores; *The Critic* carried Dan Berrigan's picture on its cover; the *Saturday Review* published his embarrassing poem comparing himself with Dietrich Bonhoeffer.[3] Serious journalists described the Berrigans as a new, important phenomenon pointing to the future development of the Church. Such diverse characters as John Cogley and Garry Wills ended their books about the American Church with suggestions that the Berrigan type radicals represented the beginning of a whole new era in American Catholic history. Scarcely had the books appeared when the Berrigans were in disgrace (probably because they were acquitted at Harrisburg—martyrdom is superior to acquittal). *The New Yorker,* which had begun the cult, turned against "Dan," portraying him as a rude, self-righteous book. When "Liz" and "Phil" revealed their secret "marriage" (innocent of either civil or ecclesiastical blessing) and was then arrested for shoplifting, the word went out along the communication networks that the Berrigans were inoperative." Catholic radicalism was "out."

Fine and dandy. It was another splendid victory for the Gnostic Devil. Some Catholic young people had burned themselves to death; others—not big enough fish for Ramsey Clark to defend—were in jail; and still others spent a good deal of their lives and energy on a cause that was not unfashionable. The Berrigans themselves, having been led down the path to national fame, suddenly found their supporters and allies simply not around anymore, if they were not turned against them. Last year's hero, last year's cause, last year's revelation pile up like the trash heaps of last year's automobiles—and the cultural forces producing built-in obsolescence in both ideas and motorcars may well be the same.

[3] Let me add quickly that I think Daniel Berrigan is a great poet. His poem about his father's death is one of the most beautiful things I have ever read.

There are two factors at work. One is the necessity for those who publish, edit, and write periodical journals to find something new. One can scarcely blame them for what is, after all, their business. The other factor is the assumption on the part of the better-educated (which usually means half-educated) segment of the American population that things are changing terribly fast, that if one doesn't keep up with those changes, one will be left far behind. Alvin Toffler's *Future Shock* and Margaret Mead's *Culture and Commitment* both represent pseudo-intellectual reinforcements of this fear. All good social scientists, of course, must wrestle with the problem of balancing continuity and change. Most contemporary social scientists are aware of the fluidity and dynamism of modern society; their real problem is to remember how much continuity there is and how overwhelmingly powerful can the influence of the past be on the present. Writers like Toffler and Mead solve the problem of balancing continuity and change by simply writing off continuity. Their books become popular because much of the half-educated population is persuaded that there is no such thing as continuity.

A passionate fear of being left behind assails many college-educated Americans. You may not particularly want to smoke pot, for example, but if everybody is doing it, you'd better do it too, or you may be left out. You may be relatively satisfied with the sexual relationship in your marriage, yet if the most advanced, most sophisticated, most fashionable groups are engaged in swinging, then maybe you'd better experiment with it too or you will be left behind. Drug-taking and adultery are scarcely new to society—any society. What may be novel is that hedonism is now justified not as being fun in itself but on the superbly middle-class grounds that it is good for you and may make your marriage relationship better. Sure.

The Gnostic Demon appeals to our fear of losing our position of moral superiority, of being swept up by the onrushing masses and becoming "just like everyone else." Our value, our worth, our dignity, our uniqueness are dependent on having access to the newest revelation, the current secret, the officially approved wisdoms. Our friend the Gnostic Demon has a great thing going for him.

I live in the worst of two worlds. In the academic community, on the margins of which I am permitted to subsist, I am hasseled by the various political and social New Believers who come down the turnpike; and in that world of political believers and religious agnostics, I am a religious believer and a political agnostic. In protest, I got rid of my foreign car, resolutely refused to vote for McGovern (or for his opponent either, for that matter), and endorsed Mayor Daley for re-election. (And to forestall any questions: no, I don't believe in political corruption.) Alas, I do eat yogurt (indeed, I had some before beginning this chapter). I eat it because I like it, not because it's good for me, and I insist that it be saturated with all the worst kind of artificial flavors. I concede that all of this may well be an antignostic gnosticism, but you don't expect me to be immune to the Devil, do you?

The ecclesiastical agents of the Gnostic Demon are much worse. My academic colleagues figure that since I am a Catholic priest I will behave peculiarly anyhow; they do not try too vigorously to convert me. But those in the Church (on whose margins I am also permitted to subsist) are convert-makers from way back. Hence for the last decade I have found myself hasseled by cursilloisti, sensitizers, encounter enthusiasts, Catholic radicals, Pentecostals, fundamentalists, and, most recently, the Right to Life crowd. It is not enough that I listen to their positions, not enough that I agree that there are many things to be said for such positions; I must also believe and join them. I must make a cursillo, attend an encounter session, speak in tongues, or get out and convert some Jews, or march on a picket line, or find myself a wife, or write columns on an abortion amendment.

I adjust poorly to any kind of discipline, particularly that of authoritarian movements, which virtually all the recent movements in the American Church have been. They demand total commitment, total, unquestioning commitment from their enthusiastic members for the duration of membership. Skepticism must be left in the outer courts of the temple. As John Shea says in his marvelous poem "Christian Storm Troopers," "My heart may be made of stone, but my head is not made of mush."

I will not forget the night I was first hasseled by sensitivity enthusiasts. I was an established social scientist with my Ph.D. tacked bravely to the bathroom wall. I had gone through the literature on sensitivity training and knew both its limited effects and its sometimes serious risks. I was prepared to concede that for some people on some occasions it might do some limited good (which is all its more reasonable practitioners ever claimed for sensitivity training in the first place). But my enthusiastic clerical friends would not even listen to a restrained, skeptical position. How could I know what I was talking about? I had never "made" a sensitivity weekend, and all the research literature in the world was no substitute for such an experience. I simply *had* to go through such an experience.

Well, I didn't and I haven't and I won't.

The gnostic, you see, cannot be content with the balanced, the restrained, the sympathetic yet skeptical evaluation of his New Secret. The Secret is Total Truth, and Total Truth must be experienced and lived until the next Total Truth comes along. The pilgrimage from the cursillos, through sensitivity training, encounter sessions, radicalism, and Pentecostalism, is one that has been pursued by many priests and religious in the last decade. They had to find something to believe in after everything else was swept away. Since there was nothing left of the old revelations, there had to be some new ones to cling to, however temporarily. Restrained skepticism or even moderate sympathy was like a strong wind which threatened to snatch away each new certainty.

For these people caught in the dissolution of old certainties and the oftimes fragile structure of new ones, the Alienation Demon and the Gnostic Demon work hand in hand. Unless you can find something to believe in, something that makes you superior to what you used to be, and superior to the Catholic masses who still are what you used to be, then you are no one at all. Not to speak with tongues when the most enlightened and advanced people are means that you are not merely drifting further and further behind the avant-garde, it means that you are threatened with non-being. The alienated person is wide open to the workings of the Gnostic Demon. He doesn't have an identity of his own; he will snatch at each new identity that comes along.

The Angel of Wisdom, that old, beleaguered, tattered angel whose tired eyes have seen many fashions, knows exactly how long each new one will last. He knows that those who abandon one fashion will quickly leap onto the first new band wagon rolling by. Sometimes I think the Angel of Wisdom will just stop trying one day, if only because his efforts seem so fruitless. His message has become trite and repetitious. He points out that the healthy, self-possessed person need not fear being left behind. He observes that fashions inevitably run their course, and he contends that it is not necessary to have an opinion, a position, on everything. There are many contemporary questions on which it is impossible to take simple, positive or negative stands. ("A simple solution to the energy crisis," he mutters.) He suggests that skepticism, reserved enthusiasm, suspended judgment, sympathetic but critical investigation are the appropriate responses to the new revelations that clamor for attention. He notes that our predecessors were not howling savages; there may be all kinds of important wisdom locked up in the musty symbols of the past. The Angel of Wisdom is not tied to the past, but he is not tied to the future, either. He does not read the *Christian Century*, the *Village Voice, Time,* or *Newsweek* to determine what the future will be through the latest "trend" or fashion.

The angel of wisdom believes that it is necessary to believe some things (relatively few) with all one's strength and power if one wishes to be a fully developed human person. But to make basic commitments to a few things does not mean that it is necessary to believe everything. The mature, healthy, self-possessed person, the wise man, takes a firm and solid stand only on a couple of issues. On most other things he is an agnostic, and the Angel of Wisdom notes with irony how many things those who claim to be religious agnostics find it necessary to believe in. The trouble is that the person who believes in only a few things strongly is at a serious disadvantage in an environment where it is necessary to have convictions on every conceivable issue from the political crisis in Zambia to the existence of angels and devils, from the trans-Alaska pipeline to the harmfulness of ecclesiastical celibacy. The person who shrugs his shoulders to such questions and admits, "Gee, I don't know," or "It seems to me to be an awfully complicated issue," will scarcely get much of a hearing at the cocktail party or clerical "rap" session.[4]

The ultimate trap of the Gnostic Demon is that he puts us on a treadmill. Our identities, our personal worth, our moral superiority depend on keeping up. But even the trend-setters on the west side of Manhattan Island cannot really keep up. Those who lack personal convictions apart from the trends which they manufacture and diffuse to the population will find the treadmill a wearying, depressing, and frustrating existence. (Why else do they decamp on weekends to their homes in the Berkshires?) The shallowness of a life spent leaping from enthusiasm to enthusiasm is utterly destructive of peace, serenity, and, one should excuse the expression, depth. But that, of course, is what the Angel of Wisdom is talking about. He tells us, "You can't have it both ways. Either you have depth, or you are 'with it.' You have a choice between enthusiastically embracing the newest wisdom or simply being wise."

The problem for the Angel of Wisdom is that no one chooses to be wise these days.

---

[4] "Rap session" seems to have replaced "bull session" nowadays, which is a gnosticism itself that says black English is superior to white English. Having read J. L. Dillard's book, *Black English* (New York: Random House, 1972), I am perfectly prepared to agree that black dialect is as solid a form of English as the standard variety. But I am still unimpressed by the gnosticism that puts special virtue on its use—at least if you are white. Whether "rap" is a better adjective to modify "session" than "bull" is open for discussion.

CHAPTER 5

The Bureaucratic Demon and
the Angel of Ingenuity

Of all the demons described in this book the Bureaucratic Devil is probably the youngest. Since there were no large corporate bodies until about a century ago, bureaucratic diabolism was impossible. Perhaps the demon was assigned to other work such as meddling in the love lives of kings and bishops and other potentates, but whether he is a veteran assigned to new tasks or a promising, up and coming young devil, the Bureaucratic Demon has an immense responsibility. He is in charge of large corporate bodies, and it is his task to take them over and make them both irresponsible and inefficient. He sees to it that no one controls them and that they do what they were designed to do either badly or not at all.

The first time I became fully aware of the existence of this demon was when President Eisenhower ordered the marines into Lebanon (for reasons which escape me at the moment). The Lebanese government decided that it was not all that interested in American protection, so after a considerable amount of maneuvering and face-saving it was agreed that the marines would be withdrawn. But after the agreement was reached marines continued to land, much to the dismay of the Lebanese and the chagrin of the Americans. The explanation was simple: the marines were "in the pipeline" and had to be landed before they could be withdrawn.

At first this made sense. If something is in the pipe, you can't turn it off. But then it dawned on me that marines were not gasoline; troop transports were not pipelines. There was no particular reason why someone in the Pentagon could not have sent a radio message to the captains of the troopships and the commanders of the marine units to tell them there was no need to land after all. But it was too late for such a sensible decision. The Bureaucratic Demon was in charge, and by God (or Devil) the marines would land whether anyone wanted it or not.

This demon has had a long series of triumphs in recent years. As I shall suggest in a later chapter it was his colleague the Groupthink Demon who was probably responsible for getting us into the Vietnam War and the Bureaucratic Demon who made it so difficult to get out. He must also be given considerable credit for pulling off the Watergate mess. Gordon Liddy's break-in was "in the pipeline" much the same way that the marines going to Lebanon were.

Sheer size is one of this demon's main tools. That students turned to violence in some of the great state universities may be explained in part by their just needing to have some attention paid to their existence by the inflated university bureaucracies. The invention of and production of the Edsel is testament to the Bureaucratic Demon's sense of fun. His work may be seen, too, in the competition within the auto industry for horsepower and size to determine manufacture rather than safety, pollution control, and fuel economy. He is probably responsible for the decision of the American government's energy wizards to pursue the development of nuclear energy to the neglect of research into the development of solar energy. He engineered the fiasco of General Dynamic's Convair jetliner, he presided over the catastrophes of Lockheed and Rolls-Royce, he persuaded the airlines to buy the jumbo jets when there was nowhere nearly enough passengers to fill them up. (Boeing is now designing a "small" 747. Figure that one out!) He surely is responsible for the Internal Revenue Service's tax forms. He can claim credit for the vast HEW bureaucracy, which no one can understand and which contains many agencies that do nothing except maintain themselves in existence for years and years. He is the genius behind that presiding bureaucracy, the Office of Management and Budget. He is responsible for the insensitivity that pervades the Catholic Church's ecclesiastical leadership that has led to massive resignations among priests and nuns. He has happily watched the collapse of urban education, and is presently convincing the Supreme Court that to support the existing alternative to deteriorated public school education would be a violation of the separation of church and state. He has arranged it so that you cannot get automobiles repaired or serviced anymore. All in all, he has been a busy and extraordinarily successful demon.

His secret? He arranges things in such a way that the people who work for large corporate organizations are unable to assume responsible control for what those organizations do. Exactly how he does it is not yet clear. We know that there is something horrendously wrong with those large corporate bureaucracies (apparently even "the outfit"—as we call organized crime in Chicago—is increasingly plagued with bureaucratic problems), but we do not understand the mysteries of corporate irresponsibility. We don't know why large corporate organizations get out of control and why it is so difficult, well-nigh impossible, to bring them back under human control. There is a large body of scholarly research—usually called administrative science—devoted to understanding and responding to the problems of corporate organization. It is a discipline which has attracted by and large ingenious, resourceful, and competent researchers, and it is no reflection on them to admit that we still do not know how the large organization works much less how it can be brought under control. This Bureaucratic Demon is fiendishly clever.

In close collaboration with the Groupthink Demon, the Bureaucratic Demon acts at the highest levels of corporate bureaucracy to influence interpersonal relationships and decision-making. On all levels of the bureaucratic structure he also exploits the propensity of the human personality to put greater trust in processes than in people and to find security in established processes that by-pass the necessity to deal with people. He certainly exploits human ignorance and stupidity, which can be found in good measure up and down the levels of corporate bureaucracy.[1]

The importance of stupidity and ignorance should not be minimized. The Bureaucratic Demon understood the Peter principle long before Dr. Peter enunciated it. He managed to get all kinds of corporate executives into positions above their levels of competence. Since incompetent people do not want competent people around them, they select other incompetents for their staffs. A very considerable number of large corporate organizations are manned at high levels and at critical positions throughout their structures by people who can be described charitably as idiots. (Sad to confess, ecclesiastical organizations are not immune from this tendency.)

There is also an inability to understand the full capacities of human resourcefulness. This inability is probably rooted in the rational and scientific approach to reality, which has produced the large corporate bureaucracy in the first place, and whose technology keeps it functioning. To have a man using the same wrench on identical bolts all day on the assembly line is a foolish waste of ability. (I am aware that many assembly lines have progressed somewhat beyond that caricature. Still it is not at all clear that the assembly line itself is such a good idea.) Nor does it really make much use of a man's talent to have him stamping the same forms every day, or delivering the same messages, or making out the same tickets. (Airline ticket clerks may be far more pleasant than the old railway ticket clerks, but they still have the same hell of a life.) Most people will perform more effectively when there is variety, challenge, and stimulation in their work—at least they do until the Bureaucratic Demon suc-

---

[1] Greeley's Nineteenth Law is as follows: Never underestimate the amount of variance that can be explained by the stupidity factor. A large amount of things that go wrong in the world go wrong because the people in a position to prevent it are simply too dumb to do so.

ceeds in destroying their ingenuity and resourcefulness completely. Places like the Harvard Business School have been trying to make this point for the last forty years, and there is all kinds of lip service to enlightened personnel policy and the human resources approach to management. Still, when push comes to shove, bureaucracies are still run "rationally," which means they are run for economic profits or for administrative effectiveness. This means that all personnel (including the vice president) are trusted to have only enough intelligence to perform one or, at the most, two or three, routine tasks during most of their working days.

Finally it would be a mistake to underestimate how effectively the Bureaucratic Demon plays on the fears of those in positions of power in the large corporate organizations. Such men and women may indeed have more power to bring the organization under control than they are willing to admit even to themselves. But for them to exercise this power would mean to create change in the organization, which is risky indeed. Retirement may be approaching, and the younger generation is pushing and ready to pounce on one's mistakes.[2] Fear of change is a powerful human emotion. Of course, some of the risks we take when we introduce change into an organization will turn out to be badly calculated. Organizational gambles can be lost; one's picture ceases to appear in *Fortune* as "promising young executive revitalizes corporation X." Changes can make things worse instead of better, and many corporate executives have much to fear. But unless there is willingness to run the risk of some changes, all human organizations will do nothing but stagnate.

Ultimately the strategy of the Bureaucratic Demon is to turn means into ends. A German sociologist called this "the iron law

[2] Retirement itself is the work of the Bureaucracy Demon—especially "early" retirement. I see no necessary connection between aging and the ability to make effective corporate decisions. Much depends, of course, on the state of one's brain arteries; still I know many men in their seventies who are more intelligent and flexible and imaginative than their colleagues thirty years younger.

of oligarchy," and it is the essence of the Bureaucratic Demon. Organizations come into being to accomplish some goals. As time goes on the goals become less important and the preservation of the organization is primary. The corporate fiend howls with glee. He is triumphant.

We know a little bit about how to fight him, but not very much. The research evidence makes it clear that most of the things that get done in an elaborately rationalized bureaucracy are accomplished through informal communication networks, networks which enable intelligent and ingenious bureaucrats to short-circuit the cumbersome official communication process. How ironic it is that the people who make large bureaucracies function at all are those who have become skilled at violating the rules and regulations, the communication channels, and the organization charts, which are in fact the essence of bureaucracy. The importance of the informal network has been known for at least forty years, yet we still haven't found out what to do with the finding except to attempt to formalize the informal and thus deprive it of all its vitality.

The other weapon we have to fight the Bureaucratic Demon is to specify the results rather than the means. We tell a given unit in the organization that we don't care how they go about doing a certain thing, we just want to see that it's done (usually within some sort of budgetary limitation). It is a brave executive indeed who places such faith and trust in his subordinates. Too many people have been brought up in the bureaucratic mentality that makes it impossible for them to work in the absence of directives, orders, and policies. Accountants and lawyers (both indispensable to large corporations), not to mention congressional committees, are horrified at the lack of corporate control involved in telling a group of people to go out and do what they are supposed to do and not bother anyone with their routines and procedures. Obviously, you have to be very sure of your personnel before you run such a risk. On the other hand, not to run the risk will yield the field to the Bureaucratic Demon without a fight.

It is easy to rail against the stupidity of bureaucracy. The horrendous condition of mass transit in the country and the clogged, pollution-spewing expressways result principally from the fact that the only kind of transportation the private, profit-making sector of the economy has been able to produce is the automobile. The public sector has not been ingenious enough or resourceful enough or brave enough to go into competition with the automobile. Such incompetence is infuriating to anyone who bothers to think about it for five minutes.

But the problem is that most of us are bureaucrats. We work for bureaucracies, we serve them, we do their bidding, we deal with people who come from them to them seeking their products and services. We treat people in our daily interactions with them in the same impersonal reserve we resent when others deal with us. We do so because we fear the emotional involvement and the responsibility we may assume if we treat the fellow on the other side of the counter as a human being like ourselves. The service manager at your local Chevy (or Ford or Chrysler) dealer may want to treat you with dignity, integrity, and decency; but he knows damn well that he simply cannot provide you with effective service for your ailing highway giant. Both you and he will be better off facing each other at an emotional distance. And we cannot blame him. Most of us in similar circumstances behave exactly the same way.

None of us is eager to have our comfortable routines disturbed. University faculty members rail against government bureaucracies; they may ridicule bureaucrats in the administrations of their own universities; but just try to fiddle ever so slightly with the curriculum or with the "requirements" and you will certainly discover that you are attacking the fundamental principles on which Western culture has rested for three millennia. What do you mean that the language requirement should be either a condition for admission to graduate school or be abolished? How can you be an intellectual unless you have mastered a foreign language?[3] I knew one graduate student who had a hell of a time persuading a faculty that he should do his foreign language exam in Hebrew, despite the fact that his research would be done in Israel.

Of course, the Roman Catholic Church is the world's oldest bureaucracy and has managed to keep its structures in the deep freeze for more than half a millennium. Unfortunately there is little evidence that the recent thaw has produced anything more than a slightly musty imitation of the other large corporate organizations in our society. The Curia is not as paralyzed by committee meetings as the World Council of Churches, but it is hamstrung by its need to have barely literate staff members from countries with thirty thousand people. The same is true of the United Nations. Neither organization is able to display the facility and the agility that one would think appropriate to those communities of human beings which are supposed to be urgently responding to people's needs, one to the Good News that Jesus preached, and the other to needs generated by physical, social, and political existence on this planet.

The call system may have been the biggest single barrier to effective priestly ministry ever created. It wanes, but it is still around. One of the things that many of the "new nuns" have in common with the "old" ones is the horror of dirt and disorder, particularly that which invades classrooms when anyone uses them after 3:15 P.M. The ultimate power in Catholic operations is enjoyed by the maintenance men, who can veto almost any parochial activity. And even the most radical young cleric is not likely to want his day off disturbed very often.[4] The pastors of not so long ago used to turn down all innovative suggestions

[3] And never mind that their foreign language tests do not measure ability in that language, and that they have become only a senseless ritual that a graduate student must go through while the dissertation is being typed.

[4] Let me emphasize that I am in complete sympathy with the need for rest and relaxation among the clergy. Vacation, days off, interludes of reflection and rest are absolutely indispensable. Still there are times when it may be necessary to shift them.

with the unanswerable, unarguable, "We didn't do that last year!" This dictum seems to have died now, but the Bureaucratic Demon probably doesn't mind much. There is little evidence that the Vatican Council has exorcised bureaucratic routine from the ministry; it just changed that routine somewhat.

What we need to do is not desert the bureaucratic organizations, but to transform them from within. Such a program will require the ministry of the angel whose task it is to do battle with the Bureaucratic Demon. Unfortunately I am not quite sure what this angel's name is or where he has been for the last ten centuries. It may well be that he is still doing graduate work at the Harvard Business School. Whatever his name (and in this chapter I have called him the Angel of Ingenuity), his task is to stir up our creativity, our resourcefulness, our humanity, and to urge us to find ways around, through, over and under the bureaucratic structures. He must keep insisting that people matter, not processes; ends matter, not means; and organizations exist to serve, not to be served. The most horrendous pollution of all is the wastage and spoiling of human resources.

The Angel of Ingenuity must demand that we be infinitely flexible, infinitely patient, and, if need be, infinitely devious— "as wise as serpent and as prudent as dove"—in our dealings with the bureaucracies of which we are a part. He must remind us constantly that service does not mean honoring every little phrase of the rule book, but rather doing what the organization was set up to do. Above all, the Angel of Ingenuity must not permit us to sink into the complacent rut of blaming everything on the "system," on "them," or on "the higher ups" or "the Establishment." While the Angel of Ingenuity must concede, at least if he has read any research evidence, that bureaucratic structures diminish some of our freedom and responsibility, he cannot permit us the reassuring luxury of thinking that we have no responsibility at all.

We still need politicians; indeed it is only the politician who can gain control of the bureaucracies to make them human and efficient and effective. It is toward the inspiration and develop-

ment of trained bureaucratic politicians that the Angel of Ingenuity must direct his efforts.

Come to think of it, that may be where he is now. He may not
be at the Harvard Business School, after all. He may be making
a careful survey of precinct captains. Indeed it may turn out
that the Angel of Ingenuity, like the Angel of Precinct Captains, is Irish.[5]

[5] I know some pretty good Polish and Italian precinct captains, so the
angels' ethnicity may be different.

CHAPTER 6

The Righteous Demon and the
Angel of Humility

Most of us live more with the Demon of Righteousness than we do with the Angel of Humility. A few of us may be trapped to the point of near madness by that uncompromising, self-righteous pretender to virtue.

Why can't we say, "I'm not sure" or "I don't know?" The Demon of Righteousness stops our tongues and blocks our minds from admitting ignorance or unformed opinion, and in this he does us the most harm. In fact he can claim credit for much of the suffering that human beings have inflicted on other human beings for the last couple of thousand years.

The Righteous Demon's strategy is simplicity itself. He persuades us that we are right. That rightness is not just your everyday garden variety rightness, he assures us that we are *really* right, unassailably right, self-evidently right, transcendentally right. We are so right that our rightness unites us with the basic cosmic forces, whether they be moral or religious or political. There is not the slightest possibility of doubt that we are right, and the evidence of that rightness is so overwhelming that those who do not see it are either extraordinarily stupid or in complete and total bad faith. Our enemies, therefore, are infidels; they are not mistaken, ignorant, misguided, or misled. They are *wrong*. Deliberately, self-consciously, maliciously, culpably wrong—so wrong they deserve to be punished for their wrongness. They are indeed so wrong that, if they do not retract their wrongness, they may deserve extermination.

The matter is all quite simple: we are right, they are wrong.

We are all right, they are totally wrong. We are virtuous, they are evil. We are the good guys, they are the bad guys. We are the children of light, they are the children of darkness.

It is much to be feared that this particular demon is a Judeo-Christian demon. In other cultures people get killed because they are foreigners, speak different languages, observe different customs, and have different colored skins than we do. Their foreignness may make them less than human, it may deprive them of rights belonging only to our own tribal members. If they are to be exterminated it is because they are different from us, not because they have the temerity to disagree with our moral righteousness. It is only where Judeo-Christian tradition and its Islamic and Marxist offshoots are at work that those who are different or disagree with us are written off and exterminated because and only because they are morally evil. "Convert or die!" is the battle cry we introduced into the world. It has nothing to do, of course, with Moses or Jesus or anything they taught. I suspect that it all comes from a misunderstanding of the personal God with whom we in the Christian tradition have entered into direct relationship. The very fact that our God permits us to be close to Him risks our identifying particular social or political or religious causes with Him. Because we are so closely united to God, that which we do must be done in His name. Our identification with such a powerful deity *has* to make us right.

Of course our deity has also made it clear that he is not interested in winning friends by force. He is a God of love rather than hatred; He wants our hearts, not other people's bodies. Almost two thousand years after the coming of Christ the fundamentalist "key '73 crusade" announced that it was going to "win America for Christ." Well, it didn't. I think it is a bit ludicrous to think of "winning" anything for a man who asked absolutely nothing for himself; he wanted only a free, generous, and joyous assent to his Good News. But it is always easier to compel other people to join than it is to invite a generous, open, and trusting response by exemplifying those traits oneself.

It was the Righteous Demon who presided over the forced

conversion of the Teutonic tribes in the early Dark Ages. He was the one who preached the Crusades and urged those admirable followers of the Lord Jesus to put to the sword all the inhabitants of Jerusalem when it was finally conquered. He stirred up the repeated massacres of Jews; he brought an end to the sophisticated liberalism of the later Middle Ages to usher in the new Dark Ages, the so-called Renaissance with the incredible witch-hunts of that allegedly brilliant era. He can claim credit for the religious wars of the sixteenth, seventeenth, and eighteenth centuries; and, of course, he is the Grand Inquisitor to end all grand inquisitors. The fanaticism of Nazism and Stalinism were in part at least his creatures. He delighted in Puritan New England, and with every new moral crusade that has swept America since then. He got the Volstead Act passed, the Comstock laws, and the severe penalties for using marijuana. The crusaders in Jerusalem, the inquisitor with the thumbscrews, Robespierre at the guillotine, Cromwell massacring the people at Drogheda, the medieval popes who denounced the Jews as deicides all had one thing in common: they saw the truth with such blinding clarity that they could not believe others who did not see it could be in good faith.

At a much lower level, the Goldwaterites in 1964 and the McGovernites in 1972, and the various short-lived youth movements in between were all absolutely certain of the righteousness of their positions. (Remember, "in your head you know he's right"?) The Black Panther's "power to the people" and the Weatherman's conviction that you could bring peace by blowing people up were slogans inspired by the Demon of Righteousness.

Those who possess truth completely, totally, fully, are dangerous. And if that truth is secret, hidden, inaccessible to the common herd, or if truth proclaimed is rejected or ignored, then the truth-possesser is doubly dangerous. When the Righteous Demon collaborates with the Gnostic Demon the battle cry "convert or die!" is heard in the land (or at least its rather milder counterpart, "convert or get out of the party").

The whole point is that, if you are right, error is wrong. By definition error can have no rights. That is what the grand inquisitors thought, that is what some nineteenth-century Catholic Church-state theoreticians thought, that is what some of the youthful members of the antiwar movement thought, that is what the White House plumbers thought about Daniel Ellsberg, and what he thought about certain government documents. It is an old argument that error is dangerous and that it cannot be propagated. The Congregation of the Inquisition, renamed the Holy Office, and more recently renamed the Congregation for the Faith, would be in complete agreement: you cannot trust people with error, because in any battle between error and truth, error is bound to be more attractive and more powerful. Thus people should be permitted only to hear, read, and think the truth. It is an old, old idea that is particularly popular with those who are convinced that they are repositories of truth. It doesn't work of course, as the Catholic Church discovered with painful dismay, but you can still impress people for a long time while trying to make it work.

The Righteous Demon justifies the release of the most vile and cruel passions in our personalities. In fact he turns cruelty into a positive virtue. (Remember "Extremism in the defense of liberty is no vice"?) When I am righteous and do something to you that is evil, vicious, vile, it is not my fault, it is yours. Indeed it is not I who am responsible for my vile action, it is you. The responsibility for my viciousness is cleansed from my soul and transferred to yours. The truly righteous person has been in effect confirmed in grace and can do no evil. He has so possessed the truth and is so possessed by it that his every action is virtue incarnate. The Cause justifies anything. That is what the IRA terrorists who go to Holy Communion every day believe, and that is what most other terrorists throughout history have believed.

The righteous person is a fanatic pure and simple. His passion for the good, the true, is so powerful that the human possessed by the Righteous Demon simply cannot accept other human beings who possess goodness and truth in alloyed condition. They must get out of his way or he will get rid of them.

Why would anyone want to be righteous? It is a terribly exhausting way to live, and while it may have its moments of excitement and exhilaration, it has many moments of depression. After all, fanatics generally lose in the end, especially political fanatics.

The dynamics of the authoritarian personality have been carefully studied. Much of the research, however, has assumed that authoritarianism is a right wing phenomenon, that there are few narrow-minded bigots of the left. There are many factors that go into creating a "true believer," left or right. Probably the most important personality dynamic is an inability to tolerate ambiguity, uncertainty, complexity. The righteous person has a compelling need to see reality as black and white. That there might be gray tones in between is a tremendous threat to that which binds together his personality. In a complex, ambiguous, and uncertain situation where the possibility of choosing wrongly exists, the personality of the righteous simply falls apart. Deep down inside the righteous person is not sure of himself. As long as there is one person in the world who disagrees with him it is possible that he may be wrong. The righteous person cannot be wrong; he *has to be right*. His certainties appear to be based on internalized conviction, but in fact they are not. The man who has powerful internal convictions doesn't have to convince anyone else at all. Indeed he may be the only one who believes what he does, but he goes serenely on his way. The righteous person finds it necessary to compel others to agree with him in order that he may escape from the nagging doubts of his unconscious. He has convinced himself that he is absolutely right, but his conviction of rectitude—both intellectual and moral—is a veneer that protects the deep-seated fear that he is wrong.

A man rooted in internal convictions is perfectly willing to listen to others and to learn from them, because he will consider it altogether possible that what he knows and believes can grow and be enriched by contact with others. He can concede the point that he may very well be wrong on any number of counts; it is not at all intolerable for him to be partially right. He is willing to admit that those who disagree with him may also be partially right. His convictions are strong but supple and flexible, ready to grow, develop and change. For him, disagreement, dialogue, exchange, interaction are the spice of life. For the righteous person, on the other hand, such activities are an intolerable affront, an assault on the very core of his being.

The righteous person will not listen to the Angel of Humility, who may whisper in his ear, "You may very well be wrong, you know." The angel had better be agile, for the righteous person may collar him on the spot and ship him off to jail, to the stake to be burned, or not seat him on the convention floor. The message of the Angel of Humility is that the world is an intricate, complex, dialectical, dynamic, and fluid place. There are many different ways of saying the same thing, and many different perspectives for viewing the same reality, and many different realities in the same situation. He tells us not to be afraid to say "maybe" or "I don't know" or "I'm not sure" or "I may be wrong, but I think."

Let's not kid ourselves. It is extremely difficult to take the angel's message seriously or to follow his advice. When was the last time you heard someone use those expressions not as a debater's ploy but as something he really meant? When was the last time you used them yourself and meant them? When was the last time a major public figure indicated hesitation or uncertainty. Adlai Stevenson tried it and was written off as indecisive; Senator Muskie tried it and was labeled vacillating. We want political leaders to radiate confidence, certainty, self-assurance, who give the impression of knowing everything and of having answered every question. What in the world would happen to the country if its leadership publicly avowed that there were all sorts of problems to which no one had devised a solution?

For all the troubles our self-righteous political style has got us into in the last several decades we keep on demanding that the leadership exude total self-confidence. It may be part of our puritan heritage that requires all political leaders to evince a bit of the pulpit preacher. Self-righteousness may be fashionable in the pulpit—though the Demon of Righteousness has worked all kinds of harm there, too—but it is utterly destructive in the Executive Office Building. Reality is too complex to fit into the simple categories that righteousness demands. The political leader who is convinced that he is right becomes after a while a man above the law who need not even tell the people the truth. For their own good, you see, the people have to be protected from the truth. Richard Nixon and Lyndon Johnson were not the first chief executives to lie to the people on the grounds they were doing so for the sake of a superior moral cause. As much as it pains an old New Deal Democrat like myself to admit it, when it came to deceiving the people Franklin Roosevelt made some of his later successors look like rank amateurs, and he never got caught in a credibility gap.

It is most obvious that the righteous consider themselves to be above the law when they hold major political positions. But we all do the same thing. When the cause is right, we are willing to stretch a point. As the late John Courtney Murray used to remark apropos of almost any American bishop whose name happened to come up in the conversation, "He's a fine man. He would never tell a lie save for the good of the Church." This is not a book intended to rage against the general dishonesty of the hierarchy. On the whole, bishops are probably more pragmatic and less self-righteous than the rest of us. The righteous fanatics are a small minority of any human community, but there is a strain of the fanatic in each one of us, and in his spare time, when he is not fomenting revolution, holy wars, political movements, or "militancy," the Righteous Demon can work on each one of us. Normally he doesn't have to exercise too much effort; there are not many of us with strong enough egos and deep basic fundamental convictions to be able to admit that we might be wrong.

If you wish to see righteousness of a relatively mild but still disturbing variety, read the letters columns of, let us say, the

Wanderer and the *National Catholic Reporter.* The editorial writers of *NCR* in recent years have been willing to admit that complexity and uncertainty characterize the world (though not all its columnists concede grayness). The *Wanderer,* however, lives in a completely two-toned world. But aside from columnists and editorials, the letters pages of these two journals are revealing indeed. How often do we find the slightest sign of hesitation, the smallest inkling of uncertainty, the most minute scintilla of doubt, the faintest thought of the possibility that the writer might be wrong?

Now I would not suggest that the human race is made up entirely of the types of personalities that write letters to the editor. Nor do I suspect that the human race is substantially composed of the kinds of people who write crank letters to authors. Still I would not be happy if a coalition made up of letter writers gained control of the political processes. Our treasured rights of dissent would not survive very long, I fear.

Indeed the right to dissent is one the human race has only recently come to acknowledge. In many parts of the world it is by no means acknowledged yet. (Just try criticizing the government of China, the Soviet Union, most of Eastern Europe, most of Africa and Asia, and virtually all of Latin America. And recently in the United States if you criticized the administration too strongly you were put on an "enemies list.") We do not like disagreement. The difference between the ordinary person and the fanatic is probably only a difference of how much effort we are willing to make to eliminate those who dare to dissent from what we know to be the case.

While we are attracted to and impressed by the person who is strong enough to admit that he may be mistaken, we are not so attracted that we are willing to imitate him. He seems a bit "unmanly" when he admits the possibility of error. It may be all right for someone else, but for us to admit error would be weak and cowardly, uncertain and hesitant. The Angel of Humility has a hard time selling himself to us. We admire him when he operates in others, but we do not listen when he asks us to say "maybe."

The world is a much more pleasant and enjoyable place when we leave it alone in its complexity. We twist it and pull and yank on it to make it harmonize with our emotional needs. How pleasant it would be too if we did not have to take up the sword against each other or thunder excommunications at each other over our disagreements. That there has been so little civility in the history of humankind is, I take it, evidence that few of us have been willing to run the risk of tolerating a cosmos which has complexity. How often have you heard a discussion of athletic teams break down within five minutes into a series of recriminations and name-callings? It is small wonder that we still use violence and oppression to eliminate disagreement on more fundamental things.

Jesus of Nazareth was one of the most self-confident and the least righteous of men. He did not compel assent from anyone. Even his apostles were free to walk with him no longer. He sought no organizational converts; the conversion he preached was a *metanoia* (a transformation of personality), not a change of organizational affiliation. That so much violence and oppression have taken place in his name is indication of how badly we have understood his message. Jesus did not choose to force agreement from anyone. We, his followers, have expended a good deal of the last two millennia trying to correct this mistake of his.

One need scarcely make the point that some of those in positions of responsibility and power in the Catholic Church are absolutely convinced that they possess the whole truth. But talk to a Catholic Pentecostal or a Catholic radical or a member of Catholics United for the Faith and see if they are any more willing to imitate the non-righteous self-confidence of Jesus than are the bureaucrats of the Roman Curia. Despite the example of Jesus, the Angel of Humility has won few victories. Indeed one would be hard put to say that he has made any progress at all.

The Demon of Righteousness clutches at us. "Maybe" is such a simple word, yet we cannot say it. Not many of us are strong enough to be able to survive the possibility of even minor error. In the core of our personalities we seem to need to be infallible. It is a painful and strange way to live, for we only learn and grow by our mistakes. But if in our righteousness we never admit a mistake, how can they ever be useful to us? The Angel of Humility has the very devil of a time getting us to even reluctantly and with ill grace say, "Yeah, I guess I was wrong."

CHAPTER 7

The Demon of Shame and the
Angel of Eroticism

The devastating power of the Devil of Shame comes from his ability to cut the ground out from under our personalities, to shake the core of our beings the way an earthquake shakes the ground. Those of us who have experienced an earthquake know the terrifying feeling that the ground might open up and swallow us. When shame takes possession of us the reaction is remarkably similar; we are afraid that the ground might open up and at the same time we almost wish it would. A novice about to make a public speech has prepared every single word. He looks out over his audience, and it may well be a friendly one, and discovers that he cannot remember one phrase. A brilliant student enters an examination room and blanks out completely, failing a test he should have passed with high honors. A doctoral student has all the materials he needs for his dissertation, but he can never finish it because of the paralyzing fear that assails him every time he sits down at the typewriter. A young man tries to declare his love for a young woman and becomes tongue-tied and inarticulate in her presence. A worker plans an important conversation with his boss; he knows exactly what he wants to say and exactly what nuance he wants to convey, but he becomes incoherent as soon as the conversation begins. An accomplished politician and speaker goes before the unblinking eye of the TV camera and freezes. All the naturalness that came so easily to him before a live audience ebbs away; he is stiff and awkward as the lens focuses upon him. The Demon of Shame claps his hands and

stamps his feet. Once more he has succeeded in inhibiting the excellence in a human personality.

Shame is a physical emotion. Animals apparently have it too.
A cat and a dog, for example, who have been carefully house-
trained behave shamefacedly when they violate their disciplined
habits. Humans know what it is like to be surprised in a partial
or total state of undress. Our reaction is a startled jump. Modesty
and privacy are involved, which are both legitimate emotions;
but our reaction is stronger and more fearful than a violation of
modesty and our sense of privacy would warrant. It comes from
being seen in one's entirety, of having nothing left to hide, of being revealed as one really is. It is, of course, quite irrational. The
dignified, intelligent response under such circumstances is to
calmly cover oneself (or not to do so, depending on the situation). Panic and awkward haste simply make an embarrassing
situation more embarrassing. The fear of total and unexpected
self-revelation strikes at the roots of our beings. Only a very self-
possessed person can respond with dignity under such circumstances.

Shame is not merely physical. While shame over nakedness is
a paradigm and the ultimate root of other shame responses, the
Demon of Shame is by no means content when he has made us
ashamed of our bodies. Bodily shame is powerful, obvious, and
dramatic. It can certainly be destructive, but not nearly so destructive or tenacious as other forms of less obvious shame. It is
bad enough to think that one's body is no good, it is much worse
to think that one's own self is no good. Contempt for the body is
devastating, but contempt for one's personhood is even more so,
if less explicit and conscious. Then it is not just our flesh and
some of our organs but our whole self. We do not want others to
see our inmost self, we do not want them to know us the way
we really are, we do not want to share with them our thoughts,
our fears, hopes, visions, dreams, fantasies; for we are afraid that
if we are seen that way, seen in our entirety and our totality, we
will be seen as nothing; we will be seen through. Shame is a fear
of death, a fear of a destruction that will come when we have

nothing left to hide. Nothing that is uniquely ours validates our existence when everything else that has been revealed shows us as being worthless. What shame protects is that core of our being in which we still have some dignity and integrity left. If we let others see that, then we won't exist at all. This is what the Demon of Shame tells us.

Shame, then, imposes on us a narrow, limited, constrained life in which we bottle up the imp, hide the leprechaun, dampen the free spirit, and kill the genius that is in ourselves. We dare not be that which we would like to be in our wildest dreams (and those dreams do pretty much reveal what we really are). So we settle for some mediocre, pathetic imitation of our real selves, because that can be safely revealed to others. We would be ashamed to let them know who and what we really think we are.

Shame permeates every corner of our lives. It makes us hold back, pull our punches, count the costs, estimate the risks, and settle for practically nothing. The most obvious manifestation of shame, however, is in the sexual relationship between husband and wife. An extraordinarily large number of married people do not discuss with each other their sex lives. They occupy the same bed at night, have intercourse with each other, and set up a barrier around what goes on in bed on those nights when they make love. Their sex life is simply not a subject for discussion; it is not permitted to have any conscious or explicit influence on anything else that happens. Of course, sex cannot be constrained in such a fashion. It does indeed creep out of the bedroom and affects the entire relationship. But since its influence can neither be acknowledged nor discussed, its effect on the relationship is usually harmful. Frustrations are not talked about. They become so taken for granted as to seem almost natural. They are part of the warp and woof of our existence and can be no more questioned than the rising of the sun every morning. Such a life, hemmed in by frustration implicitly accepted, may be limited but safe. The Demon of Shame has won his point: no one is taking any risks.

Such a man and woman have achieved a compromise in which

there are carefully limited and regulated interludes of self-display and passion. The remainder of life is lived almost like that of a brother and sister who happen to share the same house and responsibilities. Shame has been overcome to the extent of sleeping in the same bed, perhaps to undressing in the same room (though frequently not even that), and periodically uniting sexual organs. But most of the fantasies, passions, and variegated, colorful, and ingenious bodily yearnings of the man and woman remain frustrated. The development of a rich sexual ambiance, which might fuse their whole relationship, never even begins. The momentary release of passion, transient pleasure—that seems to be worth settling for. A relationship in which sex permeates their life is simply not possible, and after a while it no longer seems desirable. They might give all kinds of rationalizations for what has happened, but the fundamental reason is that they are both ashamed of their bodies and its needs. They master shame just enough to have intercourse and to produce children but not enough to have open, frank, and honest conversation about their bodily life together.

The quintessential example of shame is a woman faking orgasm. She is sophisticated enough to know that her husband's image of himself as a lover depends on his conviction that he is able to bring her to climax. So she pretends that he has been successful. She is so ashamed of her body—its organs, its responses, its needs, its fantasies—that she finds it easier to pretend that he is a successful lover than to actually give him the guidance he requires to be a successful lover *for her*.

Similarly, under normal circumstances her husband may have no difficulty achieving orgasm, but his sexual fantasies of being a vigorous, skillful, imaginative lover with a woman whose sexual strength challenges him to the fullness of his capacities as a man is scarcely satisfied by a few moments of brief passion in a darkened room. But to explore variety, fantasy, and ingenuity in one's sex life is to release them from the constraints that shame has imposed upon them; and that would be even more terrifying for the man than for the woman.

And they are so close to one another. They live in the same house, sleep in the same bed, have complementary sexual organs, engage in sexual fantasies that most probably overlap. It seems almost impossible that the power of their passions and their dreams is unable to break out of the narrow limits of shame. Still their fear of self-revelation, of self-disclosure, is so powerful that a working agreement, a *modus vivendi,* is reached in which the husband and wife agree implicitly to reinforce each other's shame. They become so practiced at co-operating with the Demon of Shame that they even discourage any faint attempts of one or the other to break out of the routine pattern into which they have settled. The wife appears outside the bedroom in a filmy gown, and the husband comments, "You'll catch cold if you run around in something like that for very long." A husband tentatively begins to explore a form of caress he has never tried before. His wife notes sarcastically his sudden emergence as the great passionate lover.

In truth, no man can be indifferent to a transparently garbed woman when she appears in circumstances he has not seen before. And there is no woman so repressed that she does not feel an electric current course through her body when she is touched in certain ways. The pretended indifference and cynicism of their response are rooted in shame. They are afraid of what might happen if they allowed themselves to be tempted out of their comfortable if minimally satisfying routine. Unfortunately the routine can become so powerful that they actually believe their own indifference. The Demon of Shame has once more done his work well—so well, in fact, that either partner or both partners may look for excitement elsewhere. Excitement is the last thing the Demon of Shame likes, for then things might get out of control.

But if the effect of shame and its accompanying terrors is most obvious in the relationship between a man and woman who succeed in restraining all the natural impulses of their bodies and spirits, the impact of shame is by no means limited to the sexual aspects of life. Shame is precisely designed to inhibit the impulses of our personalities. The Demon of Shame alleges that the impulses he is inhibiting are dirty and evil, impulses that will get us into trouble. In fact, though, shame is a very poor technique for restraining the really evil inclinations of our personalities. It is most effective, and indeed it is designed to be effective, with the spontaneous, outgoing, constructive, and creative impulses of the personality. Shame works against laughter, joy, merriment, singing, dancing, painting, creating, frolicking. It is so obvious that it is these things shame destroys that we have had to create religious systems (for instance, Puritanism and Jansenism) to persuade us that spontaneity, joy, merriment, love-making are evil and that shame is a good thing because it is keeping us from evil. Shame really triumphed with the influence of Jansenism and Puritanism. When his enemies were labeled "bad," he became "good" and could cheerfully masquerade as an angel. More than that, he could point an accusing finger at the angel commissioned to fight him and declare him to be a devil.

What would the world be like if even a small proportion of the human race felt free to be themselves? If they were not ashamed to let others see them as they really were? Dissertations would be finished, music and dancing would be unleashed, humor unchained, love affairs renewed. There would be a good deal more happiness in the world, and this happiness just might be contagious. The Devil of Shame cannot stand happiness, because when people are happy things tend to get out of control. He doesn't mind spontaneity, laughter, passion when it is induced by alcohol or marijuana, because they are passing interludes. We can't afford to be high or stoned all the time (even if it wouldn't put us in the hospital), but when the laughing, playful, passionate imp that is in each one of us is permitted out to frolic on his own, then the Demon of Shame has got trouble on his hands.

But under such circumstances the opposing angel begins to have a chance. I have called him the Erotic Angel, because eroticism is self-display, and the only way to fight shame is to persuade ourselves that we are worth displaying. The dictum "If you've got it, flaunt it" is a solid theological truth and anathema to the Demon of Shame. Good taste, intelligence, and modesty are of course crucial in our display of sexuality and all our other capabilities and talents. But because we should display ourselves tastefully and modestly it does not follow—as the Demon of Shame would have us believe—that we should not display ourselves at all.

I have been surprised, I must admit, at the response of many Catholics to my writings on sexuality. They are utterly horrified at my suggestion that eroticism is virtuous, and that the self ought to be displayed both physically and psychologically in the proper kinds of circumstance. Eroticism means sexuality and sexuality is dirty, so argue a considerable number of Catholics.

To argue that not all self-display is necessarily sexual and that sex is not dirty is a lost cause. They may know the theological and psychological arguments, but they will not listen to them. Part of the reason is that shame has become such an obsessive and oppressive factor in their lives that it is inconceivable that life could or should be lived in any other way. However, there is also a false theological assumption that validates, it seems to them, their shame. The human body with its impulses, the human spirit with its dreams and fantasies, the human person with its propensity for spontaneity, joy, and creativity are all to be viewed with extreme suspicion and distaste. Did not St. Paul warn us against the evils of the flesh (with the word "flesh" spoken in contemptuous tones)? One could argue, of course, that the word "flesh" used in St. Paul means unresponsiveness to the spirit, not the body. One might argue that St. Paul speaks of the whole of creation being redeemed. One can argue that it is not Christianity but Manichaeanism and Platonism, which see the body as a disposition to evil. One can argue that there is a difference between reason presiding over impulses and emotions as a constitutional monarch and reason attempting to suppress emotions and impulses. But the argument is a waste of time. The Puritan world-view has so taken possession of these people's lives that it has become impossible to argue against it. Sexual inhibitions are good, not bad. Indeed, the inhibited person is virtuous. And that is that.

There are, of course, the new hedonists who, forgetting the wisdom of the Stoics, preach the opposite gospel of "enjoy, enjoy!" All inhibitions must be discarded. Reason must be abandoned, and we must give ourselves over to the polymorphously perverse world of Norman O. Brown. Such frantic hedonism is usually preached by converted Puritans, who cannot help but swing from one end of the pendulum's arc to the other. Shame once constrained them to enjoy nothing, and now shame constrains them to enjoy everything. The self can be hidden equally well in total hedonism as it can in total puritanism.

The Angel of Eroticism does not demand that we yield reason, taste, restraint, balance. On the contrary, he knows that we can only display ourselves most attractively and most effectively when a balance is maintained between rationality and emotionality, between responsibility and passion, between spontaneity and discipline. He knows that playfulness between two people does not come casually or easily but only after much practice. Paradoxically enough it takes effort to be effectively spontaneous, it takes self-discipline to be seductively erotic. Shame is not overcome by abandoning reason but rather by uniting reason and eroticism in implacable alliance against the real irrationality—obsessive fears of one's own primal worthlessness. To reveal that which one is, to display one's talents and abilities, to be as attractive and as charming as one possibly can are exercises of the highest rationality.

The Erotic Angel, then, tells us that it is all right to be charming, that it is virtuous to be seductive, that it is reasonable to be spontaneous, and that it is sensible to let our playful, dancing, singing, hand-clapping imp out of the bottle. The imp may not be the whole of your personality, but he is an important part; to hide him is both false to yourself and to the God who created your self. It may be a little bit of a distortion of Irish folklore, still it seems to me that the good-spirited leprechaun (as opposed to his cousin, the bad-spirited one) is a natural ally of the good angel I have called Erotic.

For that merry, dancing Celtic elf insists that we be both charming and charmed. The secret that he has about the hidden pot of gold is that it is inside ourselves. If we permit others to know us as the person in our best dreams we would like to be, then they will find us not less attractive but more so.

The woman who lets herself gradually become the sexual tigress her seemingly naughty fantasies hint she might be may at first scare her husband a little, but then she will overwhelm him with delight. The husband who permits himself to be the smooth, polished, masterful, demanding but still sensitive and gentle lover that he occasionally thinks he might be would quickly discover that after some initial hesitation his wife will be transformed in response to him. Neither of them believe it, of course, and they will only know when they try—try in a sustained and determined fashion.

And so it is with all of us. If we permit ourselves to be the kinds of people we imagine in our wildest moments we might be, others will find us immensely more attractive. Self-revelation and self-disclosure (so long as it is not the phony kind that certain group-dynamic techniques elicit) make everyone far more appealing. But we will only know it when we try it.

The Angel of Eroticism's message is simple and clear. You are good. You are likable. You are attractive, seductive, talented. Do not be ashamed of yourself. Don't hide, don't run away.

It is a consoling message, but most of us will choose not to accept it because we consider the price of self-revelation too high.

CHAPTER 8

The Groupthink Demon and the
Angel of Individuality

In a fascinating book, *Groupthink*, Yale psychologist Irving Janis describes the operations of the Groupthink Demon. (Janis does not contend that the groupthink process is diabolic.) At first I thought the Groupthink Demon was brand new, a species of demon that was strictly a twentieth-century product, and ambitious, younger demon rapidly moving up to the top of the satanic hierarchy. On reflection, however, I decided that the Groupthink Demon wasn't new at all. He is an ancient and hoary spirit; his most famous disguise is that of the serpent, and he was certainly responsible for Eve's putting group pressure on Adam. Groupthink is as old as humankind, as old as sin (and sin is pretty old). What is new about him in the twentieth century is that our tremendous technological capacity has enabled him to do harm to humankind far more effectively and efficiently than he did in the past. When decisions about nuclear weaponry were made, for example, they were caught up in the groupthink process where the demon can exert far more power than he did when weapons were individually controlled bows and arrows or axes.

Janis asked himself the question how can intelligent, well-qualified, dedicated, and sincere men make disastrous mistakes the implications of which ought to have been evident from the beginning Pearl Harbor, the escalation in Korea, the Bay of Pigs, Vietnam—these are four of the disasters Janis investigated. In each instance responsible individuals were extremely intelligent and well qualified. They created an effective, cohesive working group and were supremely confident of their abilities to handle any crises. Almost all who knew them had complete faith in their abilities. They were sincere, well-intentioned, compassionate men of good will and good faith. Yet they made decisions which even in the context they were operating in were patently absurd with disastrous implications not only for themselves but for millions of human beings.

It is presently fashionable to explain the Vietnamese disaster in terms of the personalities of the people involved. David Halberstam, who on more than one occasion has admitted that he is one of the best journalists in America, complained that the cause of Vietnam was the "arrogance of power" of those who were the "brightest and the best." Frequently Mr. Halberstam also blames "us," by which he presumably means all Americans. Writers like Henry Fairlie or Nancy Gaeger Clinch blame "the Kennedys," conveniently enough scapegoats, since they are dead. But presidential rhetoric in any one administration does not necessarily foreclose the freedom of decision-making in another administration or generation. The arrogance of the Kennedy and Johnson advisers (if such there was) scarcely explains the drift of American foreign policy that led the United States Government and most of its people to assume that America was responsible for resisting tyranny wherever it appeared in the world. The drift began with Woodrow Wilson's crusade to make the world safe for democracy, was accelerated by our decision in the late 1930s to protect China from the Japanese, and reached avalanche proportions when we protected England and Russia from the Germans, Israel from the Arabs, Greece and Germany from the Russians, and "China" from the Chinese. To protect the South Vietnamese from the North Vietnamese was merely a logical consequence of a long-term foreign policy commitment. Granted that there was a drift in foreign policy to almost universal international responsibility (a drift almost universally applauded by the liberal left, be it remembered), and granted that the men around Lyndon Johnson were serenely confident of their own intelligence and their own capacity to decide, it is still impossible to explain the Vietnamese escalation if one keeps in mind the following facts:

1. The military, since the end of the Korean War, was vigorously opposed to intervention in land wars in Asia. Douglas MacArthur himself laid down the doctrine that the American people simply would not tolerate an extended infantry war on the Asian mainland. For the military to become involved in such a battle would be the height of folly. Indecisive struggles, huge casualty lists, a disenchanted public, and almost certainly defeat or meaningless compromise were the inevitable result of an Asian war. Once conflict was joined, however, the war was fought with the military's own particular brand of bureaucratic ineptitude combined with a strange fascination with numbers that seemed to obsess Defense Secretary McNamara. But the military never wanted the war, and foresaw with considerable clarity what it would do to its image in the United States—though it may not have foreseen the tremendous internal morale problems the war engendered.

2. The political leaders of the country had a very clear memory of what the Korean conflict had done to Harry Truman and the Democratic party. A war in Asia in an off-year election could mean the loss of forty congressional seats (which it in fact did). A conflict in Asia in a presidential election year could mean the other party's victory. (That the victory in 1968 was less than resounding was simply a tribute to Mr. Nixon's own ineptitude.) Lyndon Johnson was the shrewdest politician of them all. He surely would not make the same mistake Truman did.

3. The American intelligence agencies were providing excellent information.[1] CIA estimates of the effectiveness of our intervention and the "other side's" capacity to respond were extremely accurate and systematically ignored. Decision-makers were not let down by the information gatherers; they had all the information they needed but were somehow incapable of using it.

---

[1] As gatherers of information, the CIA was really hard to beat. As gumshoes, dirty tricksters, political revolutionaries, and meddlers in international affairs, the CIA was supremely incompetent.

We thus got into a political and military disaster. Irving Janis asked how could this possibly happen?

This is not the place to relate in precise detail his brilliant and sophisticated arguments. He examines very carefully the group dynamics of the decision-making processes that lead to political and military disaster. He concludes that in certain kinds of groups—normally those which are cohesive, pleasant, and efficient in their internal operations—an unconscious process is set in motion that filters out effective disagreement and dissent. Indeed, a certain amount of dissent may be tolerated and encouraged (remember George Ball?), but while that dissent is tolerated occasionally it must never disturb the smooth, co-operative atmosphere of the group.

The group of top-level decision-makers, then, have come to work so well together and to like each other so much that their own internal cohesiveness becomes a wall that cuts them off from any meaningful consideration of facts and information that might disturb that group consensus. Individual members of the group out of the group context may have grave reservations; still the cost of expressing these reservations in a forceful and effective way and disrupting group harmony is too high.

One of the interesting phenomena that Janis observed is that when the disaster becomes evident, the President will rarely if ever blame those who have given him bad advice. The press, his enemies in Congress, the other side in the conflict, critics in the university, radical students—all of these are attacked. But the harmonious atmosphere of the group is so important, even now, that the President simply will not blame its members. While Janis's book appeared before the Watergate revelations began to destroy the Nixon administration, it is worth noting that there is every reason to suppose that the groupthink process was very much at work in both the Watergate break-in and its subsequent cover-up. Mr. Nixon never blamed Mssrs. Haldeman and Ehrlichman, who got him into the mess by their actions (or inaction); he put the blame on lesser members of his administration and, of course, his enemies and critics.

The Groupthink Demon cares little for political affiliation; he can work with either party.

Much of the popular literature on group dynamics considers the group processes to be beneficent. In certain quarters of the Catholic Church faith in the benign Powers of the Group is unquestioned. But Janis's book confirms what many serious group researchers have known for a long time. Group support can be powerfully effective; group pressure can be utterly destructive. The powers of a group can work as a two-edged sword. One deliberately releases the power of a group only at considerable risk. Those amateur psychotherapists who think that a course or two or even a master's degree qualifies them to engage in group manipulation simply do not know what sort of demon they are dealing with.

But the Group Devil was at work long before sensitivity training and before Pearl Harbor. His ancient name was Conformity, and if he has become more subtle and sophisticated in his operations in our time, the reason is that modern society is so much more complex and provides him with richer opportunities for fiendish meddling.

In primitive societies the Conformity Demon operates to keep the innovative and creative in line. The whole elaborate social structure of stable societies brings immense pressure to bear on the dissident and the dissenter. The pressures are social-structural rather than interpersonal in such societies, so perhaps the principal difference between the Conformity Demon in his ancient and in his modern operations is that in our much more fluid culture he works not so much through social structures and social customs as he does through interpersonal dynamics. He is the one who is responsible for the decision of those in the path of a hurricane not to get out of its way. He urges others to move into communities that are built right over the San Andreas fault. He operated on the assembly line and in the production room to see that no one dares to exceed the informally established upper limit of production. ("Ratebuster" is one of his favorite words.)

He flourishes in encounter and sensitivity groups that go haywire and brutalize some of their participants.

He operates at the high levels of most bureaucratic structures. The cohesive groups that run some of the automobile companies, a number of our major universities, some powerful trade unions, and, oh yes, the American Catholic Church are as effectively cut off from information that should seriously affect thinking and decisions as were presidential advisers at the time of the Bay of Pigs and the Vietnam escalation. Indeed, if one were to attend a meeting of the National Conference of Catholic Bishops, one would see the Groupthink Demon lurking in the hotel lobbies, flitting down the corridors, and cackling with glee from the rafters of the meeting rooms. For the men who come to the meeting are by and large sincere, dedicated, and intelligent men, but something happens to them within the dynamics of the meeting in which the whole is not greater than the sum of its parts but substantially less. That, of course, is precisely what the Groupthink Demon has in mind. If he can combine intelligence, commitment, and sincerity and get out of it blindness and folly, then he has achieved a brilliant success. What makes it even more fiendish is that he plays not on the evil dispositions of humans but on their good ones. A pleasant and cohesive group is a good thing, particularly when it is made up of able, honest men. It is precisely the unconscious urge to preserve such a group no matter what the cost that its members come to make extraordinarily bad decisions.

What one must conclude therefore is that there are very strong forces within human groups that work to take away the freedom of the individual. These forces operate in such a way that the individual not only does not realize that he is losing his freedom but is convinced that he is in full possession of it and is working effectively with his colleagues.

It is easy for us to sit back in our comfortable armchairs to point out that presidential advisers (regardless of administration in power), bishops, corporation executives, and university presidents are all locked in the embrace of groupthink. But it would be presumptuous to conclude that we are not every bit as much its victims. The issue is not so much whether we in fact dissent from the consensus of whatever pleasant little groups we belong to. Nor is it whether we question facts and information that manage to get through the barriers we have set up to screen out anything unpleasant. The more basic question is whether we have ever stopped to consider the possibility that the pleasant, effective group to which we belong (a discussion group, prayer group, action group—whatever) may well be caught by the Groupthink Demon. The probabilities are that the Demon is in the midst of our group urging us to maintain our pleasant, harmonious relationship. "Don't rock the boat," he says. "Don't be the square peg in a round hole." "Don't be odd man out." (He is full of clichés, that one.) If we are dissatisfied with the group and able to articulate that dissatisfaction, we can be reasonably confident that the Groupthink Demon is in retreat.

It is a chilling thought: good groups are suspicious, bad groups are not.

The answer is not to disband groups but to give the Angel of Individuality a chance. For that angel—and I confess that I always think of him as being a sort of angelic Milton Friedman—argues that more important than the harmonious operation of a group is the maximization of creativity and talent of its individual members. The primary concern of a group ought to be to make sure that it is getting the best possible input from all its members. And if that means more conflict and less efficiency, the price is a small one to pay.

The Angel of Individuality does not urge us to become isolates who refuse to participate in groups. He merely warns us to be very very skeptical about the power that groups can exercise over our lives. Their social support is marvelous, indeed indispensable; but their social control is dangerous. One cannot live without groups, but one must be skeptical about them. Like the other angels we discuss in this book the Angel of Individuality has a complex case to make, which most people prefer to ignore. It is easy to say, "Trust the group." It is also easy to say, "Get out of the group." But the Angel of Individuality says neither. He argues, "Trust the group up to a point but be skeptical about it." When we argue with him that reality shouldn't be that complex, he shrugs his shoulders and refers us to his superiors.

In his book, Irving Janis also analyzes some successful political decisions. The Marshall Plan and the handling of the Cuban missile crisis are two. He concludes that there are certain counterprocesses that can be set at work to offset groupthink. Principal among them is the vigilant insistence of the one who presides over the group that dissent be maximized before the decision is made. Groupthink permits a certain amount of dissent just so long as it never becomes too disturbing. Antigroupthink (a technique advocated by the Individuality Angel) encourages as much dissent as possible even if it is painful. As a matter of fact, the Angel of Individuality probably isn't content with disagreement and dissent within a group until it does become painful. During the time of the missile crisis the Kennedys, having learned the lesson of the Bay of Pigs, insisted that the various people in the executive committee of the National Security Council were responsible for not only presenting the position of their own departments but for the total decision that was to be made. They sat in the collegium not as the representatives of individual baronies but as a collectivity of wise men expected to use all their talents and skills in the debate over the decisions that had to be made.

Some of the hindsight experts now argue that John Kennedy took a terrible risk, that a softer response to Khrushchev would have been more appropriate. It is hard to tell, of course. But the choice at the time was between the decision taken and a much harsher response. It is very likely that in the subsequent administrations the decision would have been to bomb the missile sites, for that was almost the consensus when the discussion began and most probably would have been the drift of the groupthink process. However, John Kennedy did not go off to Camp David with his yellow note pad and his option book from Henry Kissinger. On the contrary, he stayed away from many of the National Security Council discussions precisely because he was afraid that his presence would inhibit the full expression of everybody's opinions, doubts, hesitations, fears, and anxieties. He was furious when some of the members of the group were later attacked in the press for the positions they argued at the meetings. (Adlai Stevenson was accused of being "too soft," McNamara for being "too hard." In retrospect, if someone like Stevenson had not argued the soft position, it would have been much harder for Robert Kennedy to resist the superhawks.) The President argued quite properly that he could not expect people to tell him their honest opinions if later they were to be exposed to public ridicule for having done so. One can only lament that Lyndon Johnson never seemed to learn that lesson. Neither, for that matter, has Richard Nixon.

We are not Presidents of the United States, and most of us are not likely to be numbered among his intimate advisers. Still we all work in groups of one sort or another, and we can learn from the ways in which groupthink is exhibited at the highest political levels. There are a number of things we can do in our own groups to respond to the promptings of the Angel of Individuality:

1. Beware of the pleasant and harmoniously working group in which there is no tension and conflict out in the open. There is certainly disagreement and dissent in any group of human beings. If that disagreement is being repressed in order to preserve the harmony of the group, then the group is in trouble. It may be difficult to cope with dissent, but it is better than to pretend the dissent is not there.

2. Beware of information or important decisions that are coming from only within your group. If you are not getting dispassionate, objective information from outsiders who are not dependent on you, then you may not be getting good information at all. (And it seems to me that this is a point bishops and their superiors should take most seriously.) If your information is coming from people whose future depends on their ability to please you, they will be likely to tell you not what you should

hear but what you want to hear. In which case, it is better not to
hear them at all.

3. Finally, think for yourself. Such advice is a cliché. Everybody thinks they think for themselves, but most of us don't. It
is impossible to isolate oneself completely from the interpersonal
context in which one lives; nor should we try. Still it is necessary
to be skeptical about how independent we are. Dissent is not a
good thing in itself. One should not disagree merely for the sake
of disagreeing; but when we never disagree from the conventional wisdom in which we find ourselves (and that may very
well be a conventional wisdom which itself is disagreeing with
other people), then it is time to become suspicious.

Nonconformity, dissent, dissidence—these receive considerable
popular acclaim in contemporary America. But those who attempt to become nonconformists are often practicing a kind of
cheap conformity themselves. They are as rigidly conforming to
the tenets of their own particular conventional wisdom as anyone affiliated with the "Establishment" or the "System." They
have traded one kind of conformity for another, one sort of
groupthink for another.

The Demon doesn't mind at all. Like all demons he has a
limitless capacity for disguise. If the rhetoric that makes you
think you are free is different from someone else's, that is just
fine with him. Indeed, his most willing victims are those who
have convinced themselves that the possibility of conformity has
been eliminated from their lives completely.

CHAPTER 9

The Scapegoat Demon and the Tolerant Angel

You have got to have somebody to blame. If things go wrong, it cannot be merely an accident or an unfortunate mistake; it has to be the result of deliberate malice. The guilty must be punished. It doesn't matter whether you are an African tribesman wondering which enemy consulted a witch doctor or an American scholar trying to find the war criminal to blame for Vietnam. How can life have any meaning at all unless someone, somewhere is guilty?

It is not an unreasonable position when one stops to think about it. Blaming others for what goes wrong reduces the complexity of the world, it releases anger, and legitimates our propensity to hate. It enables us to wrap ourselves in self-pity, and to attack our own repressed and unacknowledged emotions where they reside in someone else. That, of course, is what a scapegoat is supposed to be. In ancient times it was the animal into which all the sins of the people were placed; the animal was driven from the gates of the city and people's sins went with him. The poor goat assumed all the guilt, and the people were wiped clean. It was a splendid arrangement—a little tough on the goat, perhaps, but he served his masters well as a useful ritual. The scapegoating of other human beings, however, is more than a ritual. We do not merely pretend that they have done the things we would like to do. They act out those feelings we have repressed and feel guilty about. We assert as truth—proven, demonstrable truth—that they have in fact done those things we could never acknowledge wanting to do. Again, it is a very useful technique, though it is a bit hard on the scapegoat.

The authoritarian personality we mentioned in Chapter 6 which is so plagued by the Righteous Demon is also driven by the Scapegoat Demon. He needs a scapegoat to hate and to blame (and to absorb his own repressed feelings). And despite the bias of most research that only the right-wing attracts the authoritarian personality, in truth the need to project one's hidden feelings into someone else is a monopoly of no political or social group. The Scapegoat Demon is remarkably tolerant; he will deal with any man's prejudices.

Bigotry tends to be ludicrous to everyone but the bigot. I remember a gentleman (in many ways an admirable man) with a son who was a college basketball star. In his final season the young man performed very badly. Most of us thought it was because he was involved in a rocky romance with an extraordinarily difficult young woman. But his father's comments about the week's previous game had little to do with the specific contest and much to do with how "the blacks" (this was in a period when the term was unacceptable) were ruining sports. He wasn't specific as to how baseball, football, and basketball were being corrupted by black athletes, although as he pointed out, "Look what they did to boxing." Something had gone wrong; he couldn't blame his son or the girl friend, much less himself for idolizing the young star. Who to blame? At that stage of the game if you were Irish Catholic the blacks were an obvious target.

More recently, if you are black and end up in jail, it is not for a crime you committed but for one that white racist society forced you to commit. Why it selected you to be its fall guy and not another black is a point neither you nor your white liberal admirers will bother to raise. And if you are a certain kind of black delinquent who rationalized violence by pretending that it is political militancy, there is nothing particularly wrong with selecting randomly a white pig cop and shooting him. He would shoot you if he had the chance, so his getting it is his fault, not yours.

Most blacks are no more criminal than most Irish-Americans

are racist. To a considerable extent both the Irish racist and the black criminal are products of their environments. How "responsible" they are may be problematic, but the point is that the Scapegoat Devil gives them a marvelous pretext for claiming that they have no responsibility at all for what they do.

If one reads Michael Arlen's book *An American Verdict* (about the Hanrahan trial in Chicago, which revolved around the killing of Mark Hampton, the Black Panther), or Mike Royko's *Boss* (about Mayor Richard Daley), one has to conclude that the problems of a great city like Chicago are not the result of an inadequate fiscal base, the lack of sufficient support from the federal government, the absence of funds to build housing and mass transit, and a legal structure that severely inhibits the power of city government. What is wrong with Chicago is its corrupt, overweight, red-faced, slightly alcoholic Irish politicians. Many Chicago blacks live in conditions of poverty and misery? Then someone must be blamed. Who? The Irish, of course. Don't they run Chicago?

And who caused the Great Depression? Well, if you were Father Coughlin or one of his supporters it was the Jewish Wall Street bankers. The fact that most banks and brokerage firms on Wall Street had very few Jews in them at that time never seemed to matter. And who was responsible for Germany's losing the First World War and for their subsequent humiliation at Versailles? The German Jews, even though they were probably the most assimilated Jews in the world. Who was responsible for famine in the Soviet Union? Why, the kulaks, those rich capitalist dogs who owned a couple acres of land. In Russia they were liquidated, and in China their counterparts were also liquidated on orders of that sainted folk hero, Chairman Mao.

Why am I unhappy in my marriage? Because the nuns taught me in parochial school. Why am I unhappy as a priest? Who else could possibly be to blame but my bishop.

The enemy is sometimes very specific and sometimes very general. It is much easier, though, to keep him general, because if it is the System, or the Ruling Class, or the Establishment or

Whites or Men or Old People or Squares who are guilty, one does not have to face the necessity of establishing the guilt of an individual. A class action can settle everything.

Robert Jay Lifton, one of our more manic polemical psychiatrists, has been leading the pack demanding that the entire American nation be put on trial (presumably with Professor Lifton presiding) for its guilt for Vietnam. Lifton conveniently ignores Hannah Arendt's sage dictum that, if everyone is guilty, no one is. It is not merely the left-wing liberal who is obsessed with guilt, however. Fire, explosion, natural disaster, an accident —someone in a high place (usually a congressman or an alderman) immediately demands an investigation to find who is responsible. Obviously, if something tragic happens, someone must be to blame, someone must be guilty. We have got to do something about it.

Heaven only knows that a considerable number of tragic accidents could have been avoided if everyone were doing his job perfectly and if all safety requirements were being observed. It is surely appropriate to try to discover the causes of disasters. But to cut corners on safety factors is a universal human practice, not to be admired but still to be understood. It is scarcely fair to turn those whose corner-cutting resulted in tragedy into inhuman monsters. There are a lot of people willing to throw the first stone who would do so from glass houses.

But careful investigation of the causes of tragedy (such as the Federal Aviation Agency does after an airplane crash) is not quite the same thing as the passionate, headlong search for a victim to offer as a sacrifice to placate the spirits of other victims. It is much easier to cope with tragedy if we believe in human malice and culpable human responsibility is involved.

And so we blame one another. The young blame the old for all that's wrong with the world, never bothering to realize that they too will be old someday. Women will blame men for their problems; after all, aren't men male chauvinist pigs? The poor blame the rich, the third world blames the imperialists. Everybody blames everybody else. It is all one marvelous merry-go-round of hatred, anger, guilt and irresponsibility. How perfectly splendid for the Scapegoat Demon!

There is persuasive statistical evidence to support the impression that Catholics (frequently disguised under the code term "ethnic") are the currently fashionable scapegoat in American society. A number of things have gone wrong in the last fifteen years. There was the ugly, evil war in Vietnam, there were race riots, unrest on the college campuses, and while the condition of black Americans has improved somewhat (notably or less than notably, depending on your standards), it turns out not to have been possible to eliminate the effects of several centuries of racial injustice overnight. If there is war and injustice in American society, someone must be blamed. Who? The blacks? Certainly not, for that would be blaming the victim, and one should not allow blacks to have any moral responsibility for their actions. Jews? Anti-Semitism is becoming mildly fashionable once again among certain kinds of black militants and among certain young Jews for whom it is chic to be pro-Arab. But you really can't seriously contend that the Jews are responsible for either the war or racism. Protestants? How can one blame them for anything? Intellectual and cultural elites, who have shaped American foreign policy since 1960 and American domestic policy since the early 1930s? Could they possibly be responsible for a half-mad welfare policy and for a foreign policy of international involvement? Don't be silly.

Who then? "Middle America," of course. And that means, in the peculiar social geography of the cultural elites, hard hats, truckers, blue collar workers, and Catholic ethnics. The Irish are responsible for corruption, the Poles and Italians for racism, and all of them are for war. And while the pleasant fiction is that Archie Bunker is a native American, it was no accident that an Irish-American actor was chosen to play his role. Carroll O'Connor's face leaves no doubt that he is really Irish. Somebody has to be blamed for everything that has gone wrong with our society, and the poor hard-drinking, inarticulate ethnic slobs fill the bill nicely.

In one of his books Professor Joseph Schwab speaks of the disbelief that University of Chicago students express when he suggests that the Poles on the northwest side of the city might have some legitimate social needs and problems. *"Those people?!* How can they have problems?" And Michael Lerner observes that when Mario Procaccino had the audacity to announce that he was going to run against John Lindsay for mayor of New York one of his colleagues in the history department at Yale said that, if there was an inferior people, it certainly had to be the Italians. Mind you, Lerner's colleague, Schwab's students, and all the rest who have created the stereotype of the ethnic racist and hawk would argue that they are supremely tolerant. Blacks, women, homosexuals, Chicanos, American Indians—all these are oppressed peoples, and toward them we are tolerant. But Poles, Italians, and Irish? Well, they are no good. Why should one be tolerant of them?

The statistical evidence is that the Catholic ethnics were more likely to be opposed to the war in Vietnam than the American average. They are less likely to be racist than the American average—even when one holds the city size and region constant. But who cares about evidence? As one Irish vice president of a major university put it, "The Irish are obviously lying." You see, you can only really be accepted as a Mick in the intellectual community if you engage in constant self-hatred. Similarly, a liberal with a Southern accent is, like Avis, always trying harder. His accent marks him as a reactionary racist until the contrary is proven.

And as for the hard hats, a study done in the New York metropolitan area shortly after the famous hard-hat march showed that of all the occupational groups in the area the one least likely to support the Vietnam war were construction workers.

But when you have a ready-made scapegoat, who needs data?

And the laity can blame the clergy, and the clergy can blame the hierarchy, and the hierarchy can blame the clergy and the laity. The pope can blame everyone; and no one ever has to assume personal responsibility. Much less does anyone have to face the relatively harsh fact that Archie Bunker is Everyman; there is a bit of him in all of us, even those of us with Ph.D.s.

Bigotry became national policy under the Jim Crow laws, and it is national policy now in the Department of Health, Education and Welfare. No one has any doubt that universities are being pressured to discriminate against white males. "Affirmative action," "positive compliance" mean racial and sexual discrimination. They mean quotas, and all the pretty words in the world do not cover it up.

In another society that existed not so long ago the only approved groups were white Aryan. To be denied a job because one is not one of the "approved" groups is scarcely as catastrophic as being shipped off to an extermination camp, yet one may ask whether the principle involved is similar.

I am amused when universities which claim to be bastions of liberal tolerance knuckle under to racism and sexism in reverse. However legitimate the goals or noble the causes, racism is racism and sexism is sexism. Whites and men can be discriminated against too. To make up for the injustices of the past by punishing the innocent of the present is a weird moral calculus.

But it is great scapegoating, and the Scapegoat Demon loves every minute of it. He is perfectly delighted that he has been able to create more sophisticated forms of intolerance with the phony argument that the only way you can even things out is to punish a different group of people today. There is, the Demon argues, no other way to do justice to blacks and to women than to exclude whites and males. Sounds reasonable, doesn't it? And as for Catholics, one member of the University of Chicago sociology department remarked about me, "I would no more let him in as a regular member of this department than I would let in a member of the Communist party, and for the same reason."(!)

I frankly prefer the Irish bigots on the south side of Chicago who were perfectly willing to admit that they hated blacks. They wouldn't live next door to a black simply because he was black with no reference to property values or crime. But the university bigot lacks even the moral integrity to admit his bigotry. He

prides himself on his enlightened attitude toward women, homosexuals, blacks, and Chicanos, and argues that he is not intolerant
of Poles, Italians, Irish, teamsters, construction workers, or cops.
His objections to these people are based on cool, reasoned, and
sophisticated analysis of what they are really like. He does not
believe the data on such groups and he doesn't interact with
them, so he is not clear on how he knows what they are really
like; but then bigots just *know;* they never need evidence.

And one may wonder how the idea ever got abroad in the
land that you could win another human being over by telling
him he is a racist or a war criminal, a pig or a chauvinist. You
might be able to stir up guilt feelings and the conditioned reflex
of an ideological liberal with such charges, but you will not convince anyone. It may be a delicious satisfaction to blame and ac-
cuse others, but you will never get them to vote for you or your
programs that way.

The Angel of Tolerance is in a bad way. There are so many
counterfeit forms of tolerance around that the real spirit is rarely
noticed when he appears on the scene. The case he makes is unattractive, if it must be admitted. He tells us that we must not
attempt quick, easy answers to complex questions, that we
should not seek out groups of human beings to turn into enemies,
that we should judge every person on the basis of who and what
he is as a person and not on his sex, age, color, or nationality. He
warns us that we should be wary of anyone, no matter how impeccable his liberal credentials, if he denounces whole classes of
human beings. He points out that there are demagogues of both
the left and the right who prey on the human need to project
guilt and blame. He advises us to look for the Archie Bunker
in ourselves.

And we listen to his message and tell him that he is nothing
more than an old-fashioned New Deal liberal, that he is bank-
rupt, obsolescent, and not "with it." He should move on; go
smoke a cigar with George Meany.

Civility, tolerance, universalism—these are fragile constructs.
They have been practiced imperfectly in American society; still,

two hundred years of patient, persistent effort has made impressive beginnings in this country, and the Scapegoat Demon cannot tolerate their continuance. He is leading a vigorous attack on them at the present time. Civility is failing fast in American society. The Angel of Tolerance has had his passport revoked.

The national tradition of civility has proven resilient in the past; it survived A. Mitchell Palmer and Joseph McCarthy. Whether it can survive John Ehrlichman, Daniel Ellsberg, and Stanley Pottinger remains to be seen. Just now not very many of us want to give up the pleasure of assigning guilt to whole classes of people. But the Angel of Tolerance is a wily fellow; he may yet find a way into our hearts and minds, and most important of all, our behavior.

CHAPTER 10

The Privatist Demon and the
Angel of Social Responsibility

The Privatist Devil has a single powerful theme: Don't get involved. Are there major problems facing the neighborhood? Well, something ought to be done about it, but don't ask you to help. Screams in the street—somebody ought to call the police. Did you witness an accident in which one party was clearly at fault? Too bad you don't have the time to go to court. Let someone else accept jury duty; you're too busy. Does your parish council or parish school board need someone of your talents and abilities? The Privatist Demon says, "What a waste of time that would be!" Are volunteers being sought for a political campaign? Fine, let someone else do it. Are you being urged to write your congressman or the President about a matter of national policy? Why should they listen to you? Church and community organizations. Well, they certainly can contribute, but you just don't have the time.

"Stay out of it," says the Privatist Demon, and he makes a good case for his position. Involvement takes too much time, and very likely nothing will come of it anyhow. You may get hurt in the process, if not you personally, then your career perhaps. Nothing but trouble comes from getting involved, and of course once you get involved, it is almost impossible to get out. Why bother?

The line of argument is persuasive, because like all diabolic arguments it is simple and contains a considerable amount of truth. One does have responsibilities to family and career and to one's own personal development. And these responsibilities must be honored. There is considerable risk that, if one becomes over-involved or overcommitted in other areas of life, these critical responsibilities will not be met. The temptation to substitute the glamorous and the exciting for the routine, the daily, the ordinary is a strong one. The Privatist Demon pretends that he is an angel arguing against your "spreading yourself too thin" or "neglecting your primary responsibilities."

And some do neglect their primary responsibilities, mainly because they find them distasteful. Some young college faculty radicals get involved in pointless campus politics so that they will not have to do their professional work—and then they raise hell when they don't get tenure. It has not been unknown for religious who are teachers to become so interested in "other apostolic commitments" that they never seem to have time to prepare their classes. Parish priests have been known to think that attending community organization meetings or marching on picket lines dispenses them from the obligation to visit the sick and the dying.

In the complicated lives that most of us lead there is a wide variety of commitments and responsibilities that must be balanced, juggled, rearranged, re-evaluated. What must be done with a given segment of our time is a decision we have to make in view of the whole delicate hierarchy of our commitments. Overcommitment is a risk, no doubt about that. But it is part of the genius of the Privatist Devil that he persuades many people to avoid the dangers of overcommitment when in fact their lives are classic examples of undercommitment. There are people who make the words "primary responsibilities" into a slogan and a battle cry, who not only see no other responsibilities at all but spend so much time defending their absolute commitment to "primary" responsibilities that even these seem to be neglected. They forget that a good family member or a good worker or professional cannot pretend that the world beyond family and job is irrelevant to what happens in both areas of his life. We may pretend that our "primary responsibilities" can be safely segregated from the rest of the world, but such pretense is absurd.

Thus most of those who fret about overinvolvement end up with no involvement at all, and with the passage of time everything seems to reinforce this decision. Weariness, cynicism, disillusionment—there just seems no point in making another fresh start. The inertial force of non-involvement is immense. Each passing year in which the Privatist Devil dominates our lives makes his work much easier for the next year. Why bother indeed?

But when the Devil notes that we are beginning to get a little bit excited about a new challenge that comes our way, he has an effective line of defense. "Okay," he says, "maybe you should get involved, but not now—later."

Commitment, though, the Demon is prepared to concede may be a good thing. In fact, he has always supported it enthusiastically. But it only makes sense when you are ready for it. The problem is that you are not ready for it yet. Get out of school first; get settled in your job; adjust to your wife; wait until the children get into school, get out of school, get settled in life. Wait for your next promotion; get the house paid for; wait until you retire. Not now, but soon. How soon? Well, it's hard to be precise —soon though.

And of course before you get involved you should resolve some of your own problems. Don't be one of those people who throw themselves into causes to escape facing their own problems. You have to work on yourself first before rushing off to work on others. Soon though . . .

Who is to deny what the Privatist Demon says? Undoubtedly certain kinds of radicals are very sick people. The Lesbian group, which has influenced the women's movement all out of proportion to its size, is not healthy. The loudmouth black racists who are taken seriously as spokesmen for the black community, the neighborhood fascists who get on television and reinforce the media's stereotype of the honky ethnic, the bearded student radical who punishes his father and mother by destroying college property, the fundamentalist Christian who identifies the Gospel with American superpatriotism—all of these are badly disturbed human beings. They are the kinds of people who, as Dostoevski remarks, caricaturize every new movement. Given half a chance they will reshape a cause in their own image and likeness, and either destroy it or give the moderates a hell of a fight for control. Indeed the fight between the extremes and the middle (the sick and the healthy or sensible) will frequently become so all-consuming that the object of the cause will be forgotten. Nuts we always have with us.

Of course one of the reasons nuts have a disproportionate influence is that moderate and sensible people are too busy listening to the Privatist Demon to take their proper positions in social movements. There is a school of thought that argues that you have to have the nuts, the extremists, the sick and the demented launch a social movement. Only after it has been launched can the more rational people take over. Some of the journalists who sympathize with the lunatics may lament that the movement has lost its primal energy and force. They mean that it is no longer dominated by single-minded fanatics.

It does not follow that movements have to be dominated by nuts in their early phases. Many of them are strongly influenced by the lunatic fringe not out of necessity but rather because of the privatism, indifference, and timidity of those who are "waiting until later" to get involved.

Indeed it is eminently reasonable to be sure that your own emotional house is in order before you go running off to precinct caucuses, basement meetings, protest assemblies, or picket lines. Unfortunately those who ought to hesitate don't, and those who ought not to hesitate do. Few of us are without emotional problems, but most of us are quite capable of becoming involved without straining our emotional capacities beyond their limits. And of course if we wait until we are really good Christians before we become involved, we will never make it—none of us can ever be really good Christians, particularly when we are leading privatistic, uncommitted lives. For commitment beyond the immediate daily concerns of family and job is an absolutely indispensable element of the Christian life. The privatist may be a reasonable, sane, careful person; a Christian he is not.

In the meantime he leaves social activism to others, and then complains when the others make a mess of it. The McGovern movement was able to capture the Democratic party even though it probably represented only about 5 per cent of the peo-

ple in the country. All of the rest of the Democrats were willing
to sit back and let it happen. In an era of political activism, those
who are willing to work will exercise power. They may not win
elections, but they will at least guarantee that their party loses.
Those who sit on the sidelines and complain have only themselves to blame.[1]

When everything else fails, the Privatist Demon falls back on
his secret weapon: "They are trying to take away your freedom!"
A commitment, of course, is a commitment. One has made it, one
cannot pull back from it without violating the commitment, without breaking a trust, without betraying a pledge. A commitment,
then, takes away a certain amount of freedom, but it adds more
in that you are devoting your energies and resources toward
something that for you has important ramifications within your
society, community, church, whatever. It does require that a certain amount of your time and energy be focused on that to which
you are committed. Your time and energy are no longer an option to be used in some other fashion. He who chooses to go
north cannot go south. Involvement means choice and that en-
tails accepting responsibility you cannot readily shirk. You are,
in short, caught in your commitment, and the thought of being
caught in something from which you cannot escape without embarrassment scares the hell out of a lot of people. Full commitment means that you slam the escape hatch shut. There is a certain amount of perverse logic in stating that those who are urging
you to commitment want to take away your freedom. If you
have been pressured into a commitment that you never seriously

[1] It would be interesting to see some serious research done on the political
activists. That which has been done has been carried out by and large by
the activists themselves, and is predesigned to make them look good. One
very sophisticated and experienced younger politician suggested to me that
the lure of sexual adventure is a more important motivation for political
activism than most outsiders could possibly imagine. In fact, he argued, it
was the primary interest of a very considerable number of both men and
women activists. And though he could scarcely be considered a male chauvinist, he said this was particularly true of the women. The thought of the
country's political dialogue being shaped by those who are seeking escape
from suburban sexual frustration is enough to give one pause. James Madison
and his colleagues thought of many eventualities when they designed our
system of government, but this is one I am sure never occurred to them.

believed in, there is an element of truth in the Privatist Demon's argument. But then you should inquire not why others pressured you but why you allowed it. Commitments should be made sparingly, and when they are made they should be honored. The Privatist Demon suggests first that those who are inviting you to commitment are trying to capture you; then once you have responded to their invitation he switches his argument slightly and says they are trying to tyrannize you. The advantage of making a halfhearted commitment is that one can always admit, "I really didn't mean it." The Privatist Demon doesn't like even half-hearted commitment, but he will settle for them, because he knows that with the proper pressure he can persuade you to revoke it—or at least to keep it at a sloppy, flabby, halfhearted level. In fact there are probably some times when he prefers halfhearted commitments if he can get enough of them in a given group. Then he can be quite certain that the whole enterprise is doomed.

"You've got to keep your options open," the Privatist Demon argues. Sure enough, you do; but the person who has all his options open, who never closes off any option, will never do anything. That is fine, of course, with the Privatist Demon. The man who wants to keep all his options open may make some few commitments because he has to to remain human, but he keeps his fingers crossed because he really doesn't mean them.

The Angel of Social Responsibility has to concede that there are risks in overcommitment, that we must balance our responsibilities, that we must be sure our emotional houses are in order, and we must make our decisions maturely and freely. But he insists—and this is why he is so annoying—that we cannot develop fully as authentic human beings, cannot be good Christians, if we try to hide in our own secure, protected, isolated little corner of the universe. We cannot, of course, do everything; we cannot solve the race problem, the energy crisis, the ecology problem, the population problem, the urban transportation problem, the family life problem, the education problem. What we can do in the world beyond our little corner of turf will vary greatly depending on who and where we are. Our age, marital status, the ages of our children, our education, talents, physical and psychological strength all influence our ability to commit ourselves. No man can generalize for another what he or she must do; no one can impose on another obligations for specific social responsibilities that are absolute. There may come times when the force of circumstances are extremely compelling—in neighborhoods, racial conflicts, a crime problem, a serious pollution threat, a crisis in the school, an election of overriding importance. Still, even in situations when almost everyone must face the responsibility of social commitment, some will be able to do much more than others. Some will be able to do relatively little. But the Lord Jesus was pleased with the widow who put her two coins in the temple charity box, which was infinitely better than contributing nothing. If time and circumstances and the whole range of our obligations make it impossible for us to do any more than put two coins in the box, we should still do it, proud of the fact that though we do little we do what we can.

The whole point is that everyone must do something for his fellow human beings. We are all one, tied together by common blood and common destiny. Every man is our neighbor, every man our brother. Each one of us is challenged to be the Good Samaritan every day of our lives. It is a religious challenge, of course, if we believe in God's love as revealed in Jesus. But the religious challenge adds nothing new to that toward which our humanity should strive; it simply enriches and deepens our motivation. Our religion underwrites our own propensity to help others with an absolute guarantee for God's love for us.

To view social responsibility from the other side, the person who cannot give himself to others, who refuses generosity, becomes a narrow, closed, atrophied human being. The Lord Jesus told us that we would find him in the service of the least of the brothers. That is true both theologically and psychologically. Indeed one is tempted to say that it is theologically true precisely because it is psychologically true. For when we give ourselves over to others in generous loving service, we become like Jesus, who gave himself in loving service to us. We become like the heavenly Father, whose nature is loving generosity. We find

Jesus in loving service not merely because he is present in others, but because we become like him when we serve others. Who and how, and when and where we serve are a matter each of us must decide according to our own circumstances. But if we do not do it, it is much to be feared that we will be subhuman—in fact, even subsimian. (Recent research on chimpanzees and baboons reveals that even they help one another.)

So if we are to be human, if we are to be Christian, if we are to be happy, we must listen to the Angel of Social Responsibility. We must bear in mind the full range of our obligations, we cannot assume responsibility for everything; but we must do what we can, we must do what we should. And how are we to know what we can and should do? Perhaps the best way would be to follow the inspirations of the Spirit. I do not mean the Spirit as he may babble at us in glossolalia; I mean the Spirit as he speaks to our spirit. That which we ought to do is by and large that which we most want to do, at least when we are most fully ourselves. That which appeals to the most generous and constructive part of our personality, that which seems most interesting, that which we think we will find the most enjoyment in doing: that is what we should do. Let no one come to tell us that there is only one kind of social service—his own—only one kind of social obligation—that of his cause—and only one sort of social commitment—that which imitates his. The Spirit speaks to us not through obligation but through desire. That which we want to do—when we are our most mature, adult selves—is in all probability that which we should do. There may be distasteful obligations and responsibilities that are forced upon us by immediate crises. To collect old clothes for charity may not be our particular way of serving, but if a tornado should sweep through our area, collect clothes we will to aid those in immediate distress. But in ordinary times, however, the best guide to the sort of social commitment we should make is that commitment which we find most attractive to us.

But the Angel of Social Commitment is a tough, determined fellow. He is not satisfied with our simple commitment; he demands that we hold fast. There are occasional fail-safe mechanisms which let us out of obligations and burdens that have become impossible (or those which look to us from a more mature vantage point irresponsible in the first place). But by and large when we have given our word we should keep it. When we have pledged our fidelity we should honor it; when someone trusts us we should respect that trust; we should do what we have set out to do. No one admires a quitter, not even one who claims his quitting is a form of self-fulfillment. Everyone admires those who keep their word, but it is not an admiration that leads many of us to imitation.

For the Christian a commitment ought to be as implacable as God's commitment to us. Yahweh left no doubt in the Old Testament that He was Israel's God whether they liked it or not or whether they went off whoring with false ones or not. The fundamental message of Jesus in the New Testament was that there was simply no way we could turn away from or turn off God's love. It was there as an awesome, unmovable reality; we could flee from it, but it would still be there. Francis Thompson's image of the hound of heaven is one of the great poetic insights of all Christian literature. God's pursuit of us is as relentless as the pursuit of a hunting dog. There is no way we can escape it. We are always free to run, of course; God does not deprive us of that option, but we cannot stop Him from running after us.

If this is the nature of God's commitment to us, then our commitment to others ought to strive to imitate the passionate fidelity of God. Obviously there are grades of commitment. To agree to spend one year on the parish school board scarcely compares to the commitment of husband and wife. Our fidelity is proportioned to the nature of the commitment, but he who makes a promise undertakes an obligation of fidelity. It is not an obligation that others impose on him; it is one he imposes on himself. The Covenant that God made with us binds God not because we will it but because He wills it. So our covenants with others are bound not by their will but our own. We honor them, of course, when we are faithful to our commitments to them, but we also honor our own integrity and our own personhood even more.

One hears it argued—usually under the influence of the Privatist Demon—that in our sophisticated psychological age no commitment can be permanent. Perhaps. But a major commitment that does not at least strain toward permanence is no commitment at all. If it is seriously argued that contemporary young people cannot make permanent commitments because of the fluidity of the world in which they find themselves and because of their psychological sophistication, there has not been a forward evolution of the human race but a regression. For if loyalty, civility, fidelity, honor, and integrity are no longer possible, then the human race is slipping back toward the Stone Age.

Furthermore, it is psychologically absurd to say that personal growth and self-fulfillment are incompatible with permanent or quasi-permanent commitments. On the contrary, only when the person is able to focus his energies and resources in the direction of sustained commitments to other human beings, only then does the personality begin to acquire some integrity and authenticity. Erik Erikson is a popular psychologist, yet his dictum that identity only comes through fidelity seems to have been ignored. Fidelity does not mean six-month or one-year commitments; nor does it mean involvement with the escape hatch always open. A person who is unable to sustain a commitment through times of trial and crisis is weak and flabby. I do not believe that contemporary young people are this sort at all, though I think some of their teachers and leaders and clergy, lacking themselves any strong personality core, would be delighted to think that they are the wave of the future. They are too eager to persuade the young that sustained commitment is out of fashion, that one no longer gives his word with the firm intention of keeping it.

So the Angel of Social Responsibility is one of the toughest of all the angels. His opposite devil will settle for all kinds of compromises. He is perfectly content with halfhearted commitments. But the Angel of Social Responsibility is as implacable as the Lord he serves. He does not want anything in particular from us, he wants everything; he wants our lives. When you hunt in the pack of the hound of heaven, you can be satisfied with nothing less.

CHAPTER 11

The Do-Good Devil and the Angel of Freedom

We all know her very well. She's such a marvelous woman! So dedicated to her children, so unselfish, so sacrificing. She lives completely for them, and they are all totally devoted to her. The closeness of their family life is the envy of everyone in the neighborhood. She can expect a priest or nun or two from her brood, and amazingly enough none of the rest ever marry; they become old maids and bachelors whose lives continue to center on their mother just as they did when they were little children. Her husband? Well, he died young, leaving her the responsibility of raising the children. The cause of his death? People said it was some kind of liver ailment.

This dear, sweet old lady (and she doesn't *have* to be Irish) is a master practitioner of the gentle art of controlling others by doing good for and to them. Her angelic sweetness is in fact in the pay of the Do-Good Devil, a demon who tempts us to force virtue on others whether they want it or not. By so doing we impose our controls on their lives.

Like the sweet old lady, the Do-Good Demon is an exemplary Christian. The Demon masquerades as the Angels of Generosity and Social Responsibility. He urges us to give ourselves over to enthusiastic service of others. After all, isn't this what Jesus required in the Gospel? There is only one minor difference between this form of service and that rendered by Jesus: the Do-Good Demon advises us to be so determined to do good that we will do it whether others want to co-operate or not. The service practiced by Jesus always offered the option of saying no. The rich young man, even the disciples were given the choice to walk with him no longer. The Do-Good Demon implores us not to make the same mistake, for we will really have done good only when others co-operate with us. Therefore we must constrain them to co-operate.

So you can always distinguish between the work of the Angel of Generosity and the Do-Good Demon. The former leaves people free to make their own decisions, and the latter is so concerned about them that he can never let them be free.

Crusades, holy wars, forced conversions down through the ages have been the work of this demon. The forced conversions have always, of course, been for the good of those converted. They would be so much better off as Christians; they would have a chance of going to heaven. To remain Jews or pagans is to be consigned to Hell. So, too, the forced church attendance, confession and Communion which were characteristic of much of Catholic education in the pre-Vatican Church were inspired by the Do-Good Demon. The Thursday before every first Friday saw all the children of the grammar school herded over to church, and fed through the confessionals like IBM cards through a computer (with about as much sacramentality as a computer run, too). One pastor I knew was at his happiest on those days, because at least for a few hours he knew where all the priests in the parish were and that they were doing useful work.

Another pastor, a famed liturgist and political and social liberal, still insisted that like it or not the children in his grammar school would be herded over to the church at 11:15 to attend Mass. "It was," he explained, "an integral part of the school day."

And compulsory retreats, days of recollection, and Mass attendance were imposed in Catholic schools and colleges. In some schools the computer was literally used. You received in the mail a card that you handed in when you showed up for your day of recollection or retreat, and this was processed through the computer. If the proper number of cards were not filed for you during the course of a year you might find yourself ineligible for graduation. During a whole era at Notre Dame the compulsions for daily Mass and Communion were very intense. You didn't absolutely have to go, but you were forced to get up at a certain hour in the morning and there was nothing else to do and certainly nothing to eat, so you might just as well go. In the declining days of this "hit the box, hit the rail" fervor, many young men I knew stopped going to Mass on Sunday because they felt that they had been constrained to go during the week and could only demonstrate their freedom by missing Sundays. I could never blame them very much.

The justification for all of this enforced virtue—completely at variance, incidentally, with the Thomistic concept that virtue was a habit acquired by the repetition of free acts—was that it was "good training." People were developing "good habits"; and it was guilelessly expected that, when the compulsions were removed, virtuous behavior would conclude. Priests and religious who argued this nonsense probably never heard of Pavlov or B. F. Skinner. If they had heard of these two worthies they might have listed them as adversaries in philosophy or "rational psychology" (which means psychology that requires no empirical evidence) courses. Still, priests and religious were behaviorists, trying to acquire virtue not through the repetition of free acts, but by conditioning. Unfortunately, unlike Mr. Skinner their conditioning was not based on *positive* reinforcement and it never turned out to be very effective. Nevertheless, they felt good about it; those long lines of people streaming through the confessional and up to the Communion rail were a solid sign that something was happening. Goodness was triumphing over evil, virtue over vice, and young people were still religious. Freely chosen religion might be better than compulsory religion, they might have admitted, but compulsory religion was surely better than no religion at all. The Do-Good Demon nodded in solemn agreement.

And then there was the parent who came to the parish priest worried about a son or daughter who hadn't been to confession for a long time, or didn't want to go to church on Sunday, or adamantly refused to join the family at Communion. The parent would be agonized over his or her "responsibility." God forbid that the child might be in a state of "mortal sin." If anything happened, the child could go to "Hell for all eternity," and this would be something the parent knew would "always be on his conscience."

My advice was standard: whether a young person went to Mass or Communion was between him and God, and the parent should leave him alone. If he would leave him alone for a while and not make religious behavior a convenient focus for adolescent rebellion, he might be surprised at how quickly the young person would resume "the practice of the faith."

I am afraid I made few friends with such advice. The word went around the neighborhood that I approved of young people "remaining in a state of mortal sin." Almost invariably those few parents who acted on my advice would report in a few months, six months, or a year that their child was once again a practicing Catholic. How devout he may have been I would not know, but at least he used other means for declaring his independence from his parents.

What a terrible image of God it was—willing to visit damnation on teen-agers and eternal responsibility on parents at the slightest provocation.

Another and more tragic example of compulsory virtue is the phenomenon of so many of the children of families who were activists in the early years of the Cana Conference and the Christian Family Movement. Those of us who were deeply involved in the movements in the middle 1950s used to console ourselves with the thought that it would be the second generation who would feel the tremendous effects of our efforts.

It did on some, but in all too many cases the children of the Christian activists of the mid '50s turned out to be both irreligious and highly disturbed. The religious atmosphere was very intense and self-conscious, all right, but it also turned out to be very compulsory. There was no room for religious privacy, no room for one's own personal religious growth. You were going to be an intense, self-conscious Christian modeled after your mother and father whether you wanted to or not.

Of course the Do-Good Demon by no means limits his efforts to the Church. One of the dominant strains of American liberalism is that you must pass laws to make people virtuous. Prohibition represented an enlightened progressivism of an earlier era. So did the drug laws, the blue laws, and the Comstock laws, some of which at least are still on the books. Contemporary liberalism rejects the notion that you can impose virtue on matters of sexuality or drug use, but it does believe you can impose racial justice through bussing, automobile safety through mandatory use of seat belts, and environmental respect by law.[1] It also seriously considers population control by law. This component of the liberal wing believes that people can be forced to do the right thing for their own good. There isn't time for persuasion or politics; quotas, limitations, restrictions, penalties, restraints must all be imposed as soon as possible or the republic will destroy itself.

You see, the do-gooder, be he a Christian or secular liberal or conservative, is profoundly concerned about other people. He wishes to keep pollution out of their lungs, dirty images out of their minds, mortal sin off their souls. Indeed, he is so passionately concerned about them that he wants to minimize the risk of their harming themselves. The best way to minimize risks is to take away freedom. There is then no opportunity to sin, nor freedom to choose virtue either, unfortunately.

When I was a seminarian we were forced to take a pledge that

[1] Be it noted for the record that I am in favor of auto safety legislation, pollution taxes (and good stiff ones, at that) and regulations, effective anti-discrimination legislation (which is not the same thing as imposing quotas), and that kind of effective rapid transit that makes it unnecessary to use automobiles a good deal of the time. I have no doubt that for all these reforms there is overwhelming popular support. Probably the only real indispensable auto safety legislation ought to be one that makes it impossible for someone who has had too much to drink to start a car. People who do not fasten seat belts are a menace only to themselves. If they want to be so foolish as to take that risk, then I doubt that society has any right to force them to do otherwise. People who have had too much to drink, on the other hand, are a menace to the whole community; they are very appropriate subjects for vigorous legislation.

we would not drink for five years. Exactly what sort of obligation such an imposed pledge carried was problematic. We were told (fourteen years after his death) that Cardinal Mundelein wanted the pledge because he said, "If I can keep them sober for five years, I don't have to worry about the rest of their lives in the priesthood." So great was the power of George William Mundelein's personality that even a decade and a half after he was dead, we were still doing all kinds of things in the archdiocese because that was the way he had done them. However, the dictum was demonstrably false: most of the priests kept the pledge, yet a good many of them became alcoholics just the same.[2] My first pastor, who had a fair amount of experience covering for alcoholics, was obsessed with the responsibility to protect his charges (and after all that was what a young curate was even if he was twenty-six years old) from the vices of the demon rum. In vain did I point out to him that I came from a deviant, abstemious strain of Irish culture, that my mother didn't drink, my father didn't drink, my sister didn't drink, and I didn't drink. It was not necessary for me to be watched and warned against the evils of drink. It was not necessary for me to be watched closely lest I associate with the laity "too closely." (In that community the laity did "a lot of drinking," which, heaven knows they did, but then so too did the pastor's cronies. The consumption of alcohol during a forty hour or confirmation dinner in the rectory would have made most of the laity look like Puritans.) To make sure that I didn't get "too close" to the laity, the pastor would not let me stand in the back of the church on Sunday morning to greet the parishioners when they came out. Leaning against the lamppost at the door of the church was apparently the first step on the road to AA.

The imposed pledge, the herculean efforts of my pastor to make sure I kept it (he also wanted me in the rectory by eleven o'clock every night to make sure I wasn't out drinking some-

---

[2] Oddly enough, the two alcoholic pastors I had during my years as a parish priest were much warmer and richer human personalities than some of the non-alcoholics under whom I have served.

where) are classic examples of the do-good mentality. It deals with symptoms, not causes. If you control, which is to say repress, the manifestations of the symptoms of the problem, you control the problem. If you keep dirty books out of the hands of kids, you don't have to worry about giving them adequate sex instruction. If you can isolate young priests from a supply of booze, you don't have to worry about the strains and frustrations and loneliness filling the lives of many of them. (And, by the way, I am told that alcoholism is not absent from the ranks of the married Protestant clergy.) If you can keep the long lines outside the doors of the confessional and waiting to kneel at the Communion rail, you don't have to deal with the problem of developing mature and adult religious responsibility among the parishioners. It would be nice to deal with causes, but that takes time and effort, and heaven only knows how many people will lose their souls while you are putting in the effort.

Similarly it would be nice if equality and justice could be achieved in American society without imposing rigid racial and sexual quotas on socal institutions, but that would be a long, difficult and tiresome process. Never mind that all kinds of people get hurt in creating that exact balance of colors, shapes, and such. More often than not, of course, dealing with symptoms instead of causes makes matters worse, but that only results in a whole new set of symptoms to deal with.

The person who has succumbed to the blandishments of the Do-Good Demon cannot tolerate other people's freedom. He may think of himself as a liberal or a conservative, a radical or a reactionary; but he must force people to be virtuous—always for their own good, of course. At one level of his personality the do-gooder demands virtue because of his own compulsive sense of responsibility for other human beings, but at a deeper level he cannot accept the freedom of others because he is afraid to exercise his own. To keep in abeyance his fears that his personality might well disintegrate, he fills his life with the burden of moral responsibility for everyone. At the deepest level of all the do-gooder does not trust God, or, if he is agnostic, he does not trust the basic forces of the cosmos. He lives a precarious existence with the forces of evil, sin, and guilt closing in on all sides. The doer of good feels that he simply does not have the luxury of permitting other people the full exercise of their freedom—especially when that freedom is so ignorant and uninformed. And it is precisely at this point that the Gnostic Demon and the Do-Good Demon join hands and dance a fiendish boogaloo. It would be nice to permit ordinary ignorant people their freedom of choice, but God knows what they would do with it!

Which is precisely what the Angel of Freedom argues. You can really trust other people to be free only if you believe in the power and strength of the benign forces in the cosmos. Authoritarianism is the response of a beleaguered garrison that expects no allies, no support from the outside. Freedom presumes that we are not alone, that we do have an ally, or at least that there is enough benignity in the universe so that the heroic risk of leaving other people a freedom of choice can be made safely.

And let there be no mistake about it: conceding others their freedom is indeed risky. A parent puts so much into the life of his child. All that waking up in the middle of the night to feed him, watching over him when he is sick, consoling him when others hurt him, educating him, absorbing his tempers and his slights make a tremendous strain for the parent as a person. Then the parent is told that he must leave the child free, increasingly free with each passing year, so that he can become his own person, exercise his own responsibility, do that which he wants to do, not what the parent wants. It is unfair; the child to whom the parent has given so much has the capacity to break the parent's heart, and it is not just the capacity, it is likely that he will break the parent's heart. It is the courageous parent who does not make conformity a condition for love, but he is usually rewarded.

Still, when the young person drops out of school, shacks up with a hippie, proposes to enter an absurd marriage, is smoking pot, and gives every sign of being bent on a life of laziness and dissipation, it is terribly difficult for a parent to say, "I don't like what you are doing, and I disagree with much of what you say. You are violating almost everything I believe in, but you are still mine, and I love you."

Paradoxically enough, it is precisely remarks like that which will most likely facilitate the end of the counterculture phase of the young person's life. For, after all, most children do share the values of their parents. The less the parents insist on conformity, the more likely their children will ultimately display common values. But it is hard to leave them alone with their freedom.

I am not a parent and can only fantasize about the poignancy of the parental dilemma, but I am a priest who has spent a good deal of his life dealing with teen-agers, and I do know how terribly difficult it is to let them do what they want to do when it is so clear that it is bad for them. I will never forget being caught up short by the comment of a young man who harassed the hell out of me when he was a teen-ager about how difficult he was finding it now that he was dealing professionally with adolescents to leave them free to be their own agents and not his. I think my reaction must have been rather like that of a person encountering his first grandchild—especially since for a good many of his adolescent years my principal concern with that young man was to protect parish property from his persistent efforts at demolition—an effort which was at best a draw.

I do not equate letting others be free with permissiveness. We must stand for our own values, we must protect our own property, be confident in our own judgments. The other, particularly if he is young, ought not to have the slightest doubts of where we stand. There are things we believe in; there is behavior we will not tolerate in our communities; there are ideals to which we are committed. If he wishes to engage in other kinds of behavior, he is free to do so, but he will have to do it elsewhere. If he goes forth, our love and support go with him; we do not reject him, we do not cast him into the darkness outside, but neither will we subsidize what he is about to do. Emotional support yes, financial support no. If he wants to live his own life, make his own decisions, that's admirable, but then he should be prepared to pay

his own way. If he wants to smoke pot, engage in group sex or-
gies, that is his privilege, but not in our house. If he wishes to
rip up property, he may do so; we will not withdraw our love,
but neither will we try to bribe the law to prevent him from being punished. Nor will we permit him to stay in our school while
slowly dismantling the physical facilities of the institution.

Young people do not object to standards. An amorphous, permissive environment in which there are no expectations, no
stated principles or ideals is even worse than one in which absolute conformity is a precondition for love. The guilt-ridden
white liberals who let the first generation of black students do
whatever they wanted on the college campuses did no favors for
black students. Requirements, standards, and responsibilities are
part of human living. The cosmos is not permissive. When we
make the home and the school places where almost everything
goes, we are not preparing anyone for life. The opposite of compelling others to do good is not permissiveness but rather standards which they are free to violate, knowing that there is a cost
to be paid for violation and that the loss of love is not one of
them.

Seymour Fisher's extensive research on female sexuality shows
that just about the only strong predictor of a woman's capacity
for sexual pleasure is security in a love object, and this, in turn,
seems to be to a considerable extent a function of the standards
set for her and concern about her behavior by her father. Neither
rigidity nor permissiveness but the combination of concern seems
to make for a sexually mature woman. If the father is a do-
gooder, he may care too much and in the wrong way; if he is
permissive, he may seem not to care at all. The middle of the
road is never easy to navigate.

Yet if we are to believe the revelation of Jesus, it is precisely
this middle course that God navigates. He allows His rain to fall
and His sun to shine on both good and evil. The commitment
of love to all His creatures is unshakable. He demands response
from them, but not one that takes away their freedom. He is very
concerned about them, yet he leaves them free to choose. There

are prices to be paid, unfortunately, for this exercise of freedom, but the rewards of independence and commitment freely given and responsibility freely accepted are immense. The Do-Good Demon does not like this stance at all.

The Angel of Freedom is a terrible angel. His demand that we respect other people's freedom is absolute. There is no room for compromise. He will permit us to pass laws and regulations to protect the common good, but when we try by law, by moral force, by persuasion, by withdrawal of love to prevent others from making their own decisions the Angel of Freedom must tell us that we are imitating neither God nor the Lord Jesus. But, we ask this terrible angel, what will happen to them? Won't their minds be corrupted? Won't their health be injured? Won't they waste their lives? Make terrible mistakes? Commit mortal sin?

The Angel of Freedom can give us no certain answer. All he can reply is that they well might, but it is their lives, their thoughts, their decisions. We may be able to protect the general welfare and other people's rights from the ill effects of these decisions; still you cannot take away their freedom to make those decisions.

The world of freedom is a risky, chancy, uncertain, problematic place, but it is a world of human beings. The world of the professional do-gooders may be a paradise of order, security, serenity, but there is in it no room for freedom. For the Do-Good Demon is an authoritarian, and like the Grand Inquisitor he is quite convinced that we simply cannot permit other human beings to run the dangers of being free.

CHAPTER 12

The Ethnocentric Demon and the Angel of Pluralism

The Ethnocentric Demon has a very simple and primal line: that which is different is dangerous.

You are a member of a primitive tribe. Across the bend, down the river, is another primitive tribe that commits the horrendous and sacrilegious crime of painting their faces yellow instead of blue. In addition they plant their yam gardens in triangles rather than squares. Clearly that tribe—which those peculiar missionaries from outside who show up occasionally have difficulty distinguishing from your tribe—is a group of uncultured savages, quite possibly not even fully human. Yellow faces and triangular patches indeed. With such peculiar life styles and values they are certainly not trustworthy. More than likely they are lurking down there around the river bend planning an attack. There is only one thing to do about these foreign devils, and that is to attack them first, remove the threat. So you send out a war party, and, sure enough, it encounters their war party, which had the totally bizarre notion that you were plotting to attack them.

Poor, ignorant savages, we say. And yet, in the last thirty years, far more people have died in "ethnic" conflicts around the world than in ideological conflicts. Few people are willing to die for an economic system, but large numbers are ready to kill and be killed for things as primordial as language, skin color, religion, and custom. Indonesia, Burma, Ceylon, Bangladesh, India, Pakistan, Iraq, Palestine, the Sudan, Burundi, Ruwanda, the Congo, Biafra, Cyprus, Ulster—the ancient primal conflicts against the tribe down the river continue unabated.

Within countries the old see the young plotting revolution, and the young see the old plotting oppression. Women see male chauvinists plot to deprive them of new-found freedom, and not a few men are threatened by what they think is the feminist revolution. Jews see anti-Semitism lurking around every corner, and not a few gentiles see Jews dominating many power structures of the society. Some blacks insist that whites are preparing concentration camps for them; many whites wonder whether the civil disturbances of the late 1960s were not the result of a national plot by a murderous black conspiracy.

The Ethnocentric Demon has lost none of his appeal in our enlightened modern world. On the contrary, the complexity of modern society and the speed of mass communications make him a more threatening demon than ever before.

The Demon builds his strength on the mystery of diversity. There is a fantastic profligate variety in the cosmos. Why does there have to be so many billions of stars and millions of galaxies? Why so many varieties of plant and animal life? Why such incredible diversity even within the species of creation? The responsible parties of the universe have been excessive. They (or He, if you prefer) have gone much too far. The variety They have strewn about is overwhelming, bewildering, unimaginable. One poet I know suggests that only a lunatic, crazy, drunken God could possibly have created with such reckless abandon. I asked the poet what God could get drunk on. Her response was, "The greatest intoxicant of all—love!"

A discreet, sensible, moderate God would have created a handful of galaxies, and a rather limited number of stars within each, maybe ten or fifteen varieties of plants, and certainly no more than twenty or thirty varieties of insects. Of course, He would have produced the human race in one color, one culture, and one set of basic belief systems. It would be much neater, much tidier, much safer that way—a bit dull, perhaps, but not nearly so exhausting.

However, we are stuck with the cosmos we have. The human

race is made up of long, short, tall, fat; black, white, brown, yellow, and every shading in between; straight hair, kinky hair, long nose, short nose, big-eared, small-eared, slant-eyed, straight-eyed. And their culture systems, languages, and religious beliefs are almost as variegated as their physical diversities. It is confusing.

The human mind has to simplify if it is going to be able to cope. It must somehow chart its way through the bewildering array of diversity in which it finds itself. Necessarily it begins to sort out the human race into groups. The structural anthropologist Claude Levi-Strauss (with some support from the linguist Naom Chomsky) suggests that like a computer the basic structure of the human mind is binary. It divides things into twos, then subdivides into further groups of two. Levi-Strauss may or may not be right; the question is a complex anthropological, philosophical, and biological one which can scarcely be considered to be closed. But there is not much doubt that as far as the human race goes the primary division in which we engage is "we" and "they." The "we" may be men, "they" women; the "we" the old, and the "they" the young. The "we" may be black, the "they" may be white; "we" Polish, "they" everyone else; "we" may be the people in our neighborhood, "they" the people in the next neighborhood. The "we" may be the people on our block, "they" may live on the next street over. There is an irresistible tendency in the human personality to divide social reality into insiders and outsiders, into people you can trust and those about whom you are not so sure, into people you can relax with and those with whom you must be on guard. The axis of differentiation may shift depending on the situation in which you find yourself. Whether we are looking at the whole cosmos or merely our block, we must still impose some sort of order on the chaotic diversity around us; the "we"-"they" order seems to be the most primal of all.

My sociological friend and colleague Gerald Suttles makes the extremely important point that a neighborhood is by its very nature a place that must be defended. Indeed, the definition of a neighborhood is an area that we defend.[1] We defend it simply because it is the place where our kind of people live. It is a segment of turf that is ours; it is the place where we can relax and be ourselves, as over against other places where we must be on guard. Social policy that ignores this characteristic of the neighborhood—and most American social policy does—is bound to run into antagonisms which non-neighborhood people find totally incomprehensible.

But the non-neighborhood types are as prone as anyone else to divide social reality into the "we" and the "they." In their case, the "we" may be the cosmopolitan sophisticates who live in high-rise apartment buildings and who believe that neighborhoods are part of a tribal past. For these people the "they" are the poor, benighted ethnics who have yet to realize that the neighborhood is dead.

It is the combination of profligate diversity and the need for humans to devise a chart through that diversity that gives the Ethnocentric Demon his chance. It is not merely that the "they" are set over against the "we," it is that "they" are bad and "we" are good. "They" are threatening us and "we" must defend ourselves; "they" are different from us and hence inferior.

When we dichotomize humans into "we" and "they" we program ourselves for two responses—fear and fascination. By their very difference "they" are both fascinating and threatening, and whether it is a different sex or ethnic group the choice of whether we let fascination or fear dominate our response is left to us. The Ethnocentric Demon warns us to be afraid; the Pluralist Angel urges us to enjoy.

Ethnocentrism is a bigotry. If we are afraid of others and they are perceived as threatening us, then we must defend ourselves. To rationalize our defense, we need a set of explanations for their behavior. These explanations almost necessarily insist on their inferiority. The Ethnocentric Demon finds his natural ally

[1] See *The Social Order of the Slum: Ethnicity and Territory in the Inner City.* Chicago: University of Chicago Press, 1968.

under such circumstances to be the Scapegoat Demon. If you can turn the others into a stereotype, then they make a perfect scapegoat, for they are not merely inferior and somehow less than human, they are also to blame for most if not all of your problems. The sensible thing is to eliminate them or to at least keep them down. Under no circumstances may they be permitted to gain the upper hand.

In the United States the most powerful form of ethnocentrism has always been racial, a legacy of the ugly institution of slavery. While racism seems almost universal in the world (when the "other" race is represented in such numbers as to be more than a curiosity), it is worse in the United States because of the slave trade, slavery, and the post-Civil War feudalism of the South—a feudalism which was transformed but not notably improved when large numbers of blacks began to migrate to the urban North. Legal racism has virtually been eliminated in the United States; economic racism is slowly diminishing (though the effects of hundreds of years of oppression are still certainly felt); social racism may also be moderating.[2] The picture is complicated still more by the fact that there is an understandable and probably inevitable reaction to white racism in the form of black racism.

Anti-Semitism is a more elusive form of American ethnocentrism. All the indications are that it has diminished notably in the last three decades, yet many Jews, with the memory of the holocaust in mind, are still suspicious and vigilant; there are signs that among some black militants and certain radical young Jews anti-Semitism is increasing.

It is also argued by many in the women's movement that sexism is a form of ethnocentrism. There is no reason to doubt that women have been the object of systematic discrimination in

[2] This is difficult to measure, because certain kinds of "fashionable" behavior are in fact disguises for a much deeper and unacknowledged variety of racism. Some black scholars, for example, have pointed out that the insistence of some white liberals on quotas for blacks implies that blacks are not good enough to make it on their own, and that excessive permissiveness for black students in the university environment is based on the notion that they can't be expected to gain the same achievement level as white students.

American society and that that discrimination has been increased by stereotypes. So-called male chauvinism certainly seems to be a variety of ethnocentrism, although it is surely ethnocentrism with a difference, if only because of the intimate nature of the man-woman relationship. But the Ethnocentric Demon is certainly flexible enough to claim all the credit he can for the discrimination against women and to do all he can to see that it continues.

Finally, there is the most subtle of all American ethnocentrisms, nativism. The nativist distrusts foreigners, and who the foreigners are depends upon who he is. For all practical purposes they may represent any immigrant group that came after his. Although the principal victims of nativism have been Catholics and Orientals, I am convinced that much of the attempt to scapegoat the ethnics for the Vietnam War and racism is in fact a manifestation of powerful residual nativism in American society. The Ethnocentric Demon and the Scapegoat Demon collaborated splendidly on this one. Nativism, unlike sexism, racism, and anti-Semitism, has never really been smoked out into the open. It still lurks just beneath the surface of the American body politic and social.

The wife of a distinguished demographer recently wrote an article in the New York *Times Magazine* that vigorously advocated the position of much stricter immigration barriers. She told how cheated she felt when the previous year in a hospital room she found herself being examined by a "foreign" doctor (apparently either a Filipino or a Taiwanese. The medical schools in those countries are so inferior to the American ones that it did not seem right for an American patient to be exposed to the risk of being taken care of by such a doctor). It never occurred to the good lady, I am sure, that previous generations of Americans would have reacted with similar horror to discover they were being examined by an Irish or an Italian or a Polish doctor. Indeed, I wonder how much at ease she would have felt if the doctor had had a Slavic name. He probably would have gone to a Catholic medical school, and everyone knows how bad they are! Nor did it occur to her apparently that for many people of the United States the choice was not between a clean-cut white American Anglo-Saxon (and you can be white Anglo-Saxon and still be Jewish or black) and a shifty-eyed Oriental doctor but between an immigrant from the Philippines or Taiwan and no doctor at all.

She recounted with horror the tale that one graduating class from a Taiwanese medical school entered a jet and flew en masse to the United States. Can one imagine that? A whole jetload of Orientals streaming into the American medical profession? One can imagine exactly the same horror of the prim New York ladies watching the sailing ships disgorge huge cargoes of sloppy, dirty, brawling, drunken Irishmen.

Nativism is the real pride and joy of the Ethnocentric Demon. He must dread the day when it is finally smoked out and called by its proper name.

The ethnocentric tendency is strong and practically universal. The "they" whom we fear and stereotype and scapegoat may vary, depending on who we are; but everyone has his "they" available. It is even possible for the "they" to be our own ancestors, for ethnocentrism can be temporal as well as spatial. There is a certain kind of writer who thinks that everyone who lived before Sigmund Freud was a howling savage. Our own era, with its "freedom from dogma," its refusal to be trapped in rigidities, its "openness," is seen as the hinge of history—a hinge which is in fact really just the beginning of meaningful history. The eighteenth-century Enlightenment with its rationalism is the grandparent of ethnocentrism, and the conviction that a New Age has begun is much older. So the Freudians, particularly the pop variety, are merely the latest to think that they have begun the Age of the Holy Spirit.[3] It is interesting to note that the heirs to one of the longest and grandest traditions in human history—theologians, church leaders and clergy—have joined

[3] The Freudians are not alone. B. F. Skinner and Charles Reich seem to think the same thing.

the ranks of the future-worshipers and have written off everything that happened before 1925. The advice of Jaraslav Pelikan
that when we sit down around the table to discuss theology we
should include not only the best representatives of our own age
but also the best of the past is quite unacceptable to these
churchmen.

I find temporal ethnocentrists even more contemptible than
spatial ethnocentrists, for at least the stereotyped group among
your own contemporaries is alive and able to fight back. Stereotypes and scapegoats out of the past cannot defend themselves.
Downgrading them is like blasting ducks at a shooting gallery.

The Angel of Diversity responds to the ethnocentric question
"Why can't they be like us?"[4] with the perfectly obvious and
sensible answer that *they* are not going to become like us; they
will not acquire our sex, our race, our culture, our language, and
very likely not our religion either. "They" will continue to be different and there is nothing much we can do to change them. So
instead of trying to eliminate diversity we should settle down
and begin to enjoy it—which is apparently what the Deity had in
mind when he created this wild cosmos of His.

But the Ethnocentric Demon has a powerful response, one
that is particularly dear to his favorite pupil, the American nativist: most of the trouble we have in the world comes from
diversity. There is already too much diversity in the United
States. We should strive to diminish it so that there might be
national unity. The heterogeneity of our society threatens to tear
it apart.

A similar argument is advocated by those who insisted on national uniformity within the Catholic Church. You had to keep
the liturgy and the laws and the language of the Church the
same everywhere, otherwise you might "encourage nationalism."
As it was, we were told, everywhere in the world you went you

---

[4] Any similarity between this question and a book published by Dutton in
1971 is purely accidental. (Editor's Note: Not accidental is the fact that the
author is Andrew M. Greeley.)

would hear Mass in the same language—a language that nobody anywhere understood or spoke.[5]

The nativist's rejection of diversity and pluralism is unanswerable not because it is a solidly argued position but because the nativist will admit of no counterargument. The fact that American society when compared to others has held together remarkably well, given its pluralism, is amazing. The nativist is also never very clear on how one might go about eliminating the diversity that so obviously exists in our society, nor does he provide us with a model toward which we should be moving in the process of homogenization (and it is not clear that homogeneous countries like Sweden and France, for example, are free from drastic internal strains and tension). But the pious warnings of the assimilationists are a waste of time. Social harmony is not achieved by homogenization but by integration, an integration that leaves wide room for diversity. The question is not how are we to harmonize? but how are we to combine unity and pluralism? Such a combination will never be achieved by pretending that the diversity which exists and shows no particular sign of waning just isn't there anymore.

I am very skeptical of most of the social "trends" one reads about in the social science books, but I think pluralism may well be one of the major trends of our time. By pluralism I do not mean a permissiveness that says it doesn't matter what people do, nor a relativism that says that one has no convictions at all. It is rather a willingness to let other cultures, different values, different aspirations, and different goals exist within their own contexts. This pluralistic development is a very broad phenomenon that includes religious belief, ethnic and racial cultures, political attitudes, life-styles, values, and goals. It permits others to do pretty much what they want to do, so long as they do not threaten other people in the society. More than that, I see in this pluralistic strain a willingness to listen to, learn from, and enjoy

[5] The argument was phony, because before the Vatican Council Mass was said in at least twenty languages—most of which, if the truth be told, no one could understand.

the life-styles and the cultural, political, and intellectual differences it sees around it. We are becoming able to enjoy Indian
jewelry, Italian food, black language, Irish and Jewish humor
without giving up our own convictions or life-styles. There is obviously a fair amount of dilettantism in this new acceptance of
diversity, but a dilettante can be serious and sophisticated.

I should not like to see this strain toward pluralism applauded
as some great and enlightened evolutionary leap forward. It is
probably much more the result of an economic prosperity that
gives us enough financial security to permit our fascination with
that which is different from us some room to operate. Still the
Pluralistic Angel, who has had a hard enough time of it throughout most of the history of the human race, will settle for almost
any change no matter how material its base.

It may be that humankind, in its lurching, groping, erratic
advance down the corridors of history, has finally begun to find
the intellectual and economic resources to make the enjoyment of
diversity somewhat easier than before. Ethnocentrism has by no
means vanished. The television screen and the jet airplane have
not necessarily made us more tolerant of the diversity in humankind. Prejudice and bigotry are like prairie fires: you damp one
down and another breaks out somewhere else. Still the atmosphere is probably more conducive to pluralism now than ever before in human history. That may not be much of an improvement, but it is something. That it is even a little easier for us now
to emphasize the fascination of the different rather than its terror
opens up vast new opportunities for joy, enrichment, and happiness in the human condition. If it is all right for others not to be
like us, then we can listen to them, enjoy them, profit from their
contribution, and maybe even learn something from them. The
Ethnocentric Demon, who has had things his own way for so long,
will be stamping his feet in anger.

CHAPTER 13

The Ideological Demon and the Angel of Pragmatism

Ideology, according to the distinguished anthropologist Clifford Geertz, is a symbol system that enables one to chart one's way through political confusion and chaos. In his classic article "Ideology as a Culture System,"[1] Geertz offers the example of the Taft-Hartley Law.[2] Labor union leadership vigorously opposed the law because they were not sure how effective it would be and partly because the arguments buttressing it were fallacious. But it was an extremely complex law and the arguments against it were necessarily complex. In order to rally the rank and file union members against the legislation, a good shorthand description was required. The union leaders settled for the phrase "slave labor law," mostly because the American public was at that time becoming aware of the slave labor camps in the Soviet Union. No one, union leaders, rank and file, Truman administration, or supporters of the bill, took the slogan with literal seriousness. Obviously, Senator Taft and Representative Hartley did not plan to establish slave labor camps here. The most they intended to do was to inhibit trade unionism and tip the scales in favor of business management. The slogan "slave labor law" conveyed the fundamental antilabor bias which the union leadership saw in the proposed legislation.

Well, the act was passed and remains on the books. Unions,

[1] In David E. Apter (ed.), *Ideology and Discontent*. New York: The Free Press, 1964, pp. 62–63.
[2] An antilabor bill put through the U. S. Congress in the late 1940s. It was described by one wit as "hell for unions, purgatory for management, and heaven for lawyers."

while hampered, continue to exist. Whether the symbol was effective or not in rallying rank and file opposition to the legislation is dubious, but it was in any case an exercise in ideology. It compressed arguments, feelings, emotions, fears, aspirations into one rich symbol around which at least some of the workingmen in America were able to rally in opposition to the bill. Taken literally, it was absurd; taken as a symbol, it conveyed a message of considerable impact at a time of doubt and confusion within the American labor movement.

If the symbol had been taken literally by even a substantial minority of the American trade movement and unionists really believed that the government was preparing labor camps in the hills of South Dakota, then we may very well have had violent demonstrations at least. But ideological symbols are just figurative, imaginative ways of saying something important and passionate about social reality. What they say is true enough at a symbolic level, but if they are interpreted literally, they can become devilishly dangerous.

And this is precisely what the Ideological Demon has in mind. The campaign slogans of Republican and Democratic politicians of the regular professional variety are perfectly useless to him. He knows that they will not be taken literally; they are not intended literally. They are means of communication and, perhaps in some instances, a moderately effective means to the party faithful at least. Ideology becomes dangerous only when the symbols are translated into a complex, systematic set of propositions which purport to give both total analysis of the situation and total solution to its problems. This kind of ideology—one might call it "systematic ideology"—is the sort of thing that gives the Ideological Demon a field day.

It is especially to intellectuals, those who earn their livings by the manipulation of words and with their minds, that systematic ideology has its greatest appeal. Their intellects and the capacity for propositional expression have been elaborately developed and refined. Reality for them exists in their verbal descriptions of it. Understanding is the same as labeling. If you can give a name to something, you have coped with it. System, order, neatness, precision, eloquence—these are the intellectual's stock in trade. Hence when he approaches the complex, messy, confusing, disorderly world of political and social life, he tries to put system and order into it. The ideological symbols give him a vision, and he resolutely and rigorously applies his vision to the political and social world he observes. The classic combination of visionary and intellectual ideologue was Karl Marx. He saw a vision of oppression, and in the struggles of the working class he saw a symbol of resistance to that oppression. Then, with marvelous Teutonic efficiency and remarkable intellectual ingenuity, he developed a systematic analysis of and detailed prescription for remedying the plight of the workingman. In the century and a quarter since the *Communist Manifesto*—that quintessential combination of symbolic vision and intellectual system—Marx's world view has exercised an almost irresistible fascination for intellectuals. And this despite the fact that, wherever those who have ascribed to that world view have taken power, freedom vanishes and the worst sorts of tyranny and oppression supplant it.[3] It is problematic that when communist revolutionaries seize power they do very much to improve the lot of the workingman, but it is not problematic that the workingman gains power; he surely does not. Others exercise power in his name without his consent. If he bothers to object he is likely to end up in Siberia or in a "re-education center" in China or, if worse comes to worse, in front of a firing squad. (These days, he may be sent to a mental institution—an interesting admission of the psychological element in economically determined social history. Marx updated in the post-Freudian world.)

But regardless of the failings of Marxism in practice, the theory of Marxism is so elaborate, so complex, so elegant, so neat,

[3] The social democratic parties in Western Europe can scarcely be considered Marxist in even the most abstract sense. They are middle-class liberal democratic parties rooted in the French Revolution far more securely than in the *Communist Manifesto*.

so tidy, so incisive, so useful for ordering data that its fascination for the intellectual continues unabated.[4]

Systematic ideologies will continue to attract intellectuals as long as scholarly training tends to overdevelop cognitive and discursive intellect in relation to other forms of cognition and expression. In the absence of a different kind of intellectual training or a return to religious belief by our present breed of hypercognitive intellectuals, ideology will flourish.

Ideology will have impact on ordinary people, as Geertz suggests, only in times of confusion, unrest, and uncertainty. But what will attract ordinary people is not the complex, philosophical, and social scientific (or pseudosocial scientific) systems that the intellectuals have put together. What will attract them are the powerful, symbolic slogans which express the core of the ideology. In 1917 when the Russian Empire and its army were falling apart, it was not dialectical materialism that won some of the population to the Bolsheviks but their simple slogan, "bread, land, peace." Lenin was an intellectual with a very definite feeling for people and situations—at least how to manipulate them.

And in time of unrest and uncertainty in the Weimar Republic of Germany, after Versailles and during the Great Depression, it was not the half-mad system of *Mein Kampf* that attracted the people to the Nazis, rather it was Hitler's reverence for the "Fatherland" and his promise to restore order and dignity to the German nation.

The radical right in the United States in the forties and fifties were pretty much without system and coherence, but they rallied around such leaders as the late Senator McCarthy precisely because he gave voice to their unease as they saw the balance of power shift from rural Protestant America to urban alien America. (That McCarthy was an Irish Catholic is one of the ironies

---

[4] One might well distinguish between Marxist economic and historical analysis, some of which is extremely useful, and Marxism as an ideological system, which analyzes contemporary problems and prescribes solutions for them. This is not a distinction that Marxist intellectuals like to make before they come to power, and, of course, after they assume power they become members of the New Class and are beyond criticism.

of the situation.) Similarly, the shorter-lived New Left of the late sixties had nothing more elaborate than the gibberish of the Port Huron Statement, but its symbols of a "sick," "imperialist" America were useful charts through which young activists and not so young professors and journalists could find a way in the midst of the confusions and uncertainties in the wake of the Kennedy assassination and the urban riots and the Vietnam War.

The distinguished sociologist Daniel Bell argued just before the sixties began that we were at an end of ideology. He concluded that ideological response to social problems (by which he meant a Marxist response) was no longer viable, that experts, technicians, and intellectuals of the pragmatic, problem-oriented variety would solve the remaining social problems of the country. Those members of the New Left—and Bell's old enemies from the interminable Marxist factional feuds of Manhattan and Cambridge of the 1930s and '40s—have never let him forget how wrong his prediction was. For there was a rebirth of ideology, no matter how thin and shallow it may have been, and at least some of it still lingers. Indeed the ideologues became so powerful that they were able to do what the Old Left never did in the 1930s, they were able to capture the Democratic party and nominate their own front man for the presidency. Whereupon he was promptly buried by one of the most unattractive candidates of the twentieth century.

But Bell was probably right in the long run. Ideologies will get mass support (by which I mean millions, not tens of millions) in the United States only in times of crisis and unrest. Otherwise they will remain pleasant games for intellectuals to play. The New Left may have managed to re-elect Richard Nixon, but beyond that it had little effect on the political and economic life of America. It may have had some effect on lifestyles. The dress and manners chosen by the New Left students of the mid-sixties quickly spread throughout the country, but such is the nature of a consumer society that when the masses take on the fashions of the intellectual ideologues, they remove from it most of the original meaning. When a steelworker from

Gary or a professional football player from Texas wears long hair and sideburns, it is not quite the same thing as when a radical student refused to cut his hair in the early 1960s. If all the left can do in the country is to establish fashions in clothes and hair styles and influence the sex lives of a small segment of the population, it is pretty much a failure.

The intellectual ideologue, as he manifested himself in the late sixties, has now been rather effectively defused. Public policy, it would appear, will continue to be made not by the academics, with their elegance of analysis and expression, and by their imitators in the world of *haute* journalism, but by politicians who have a "feel" for what they can and cannot do and for what will work and what will not. Both politicians and intellectuals make mistakes, but by and large, however, I suspect that the mistakes of the politicians are less serious. They are less likely to dig themselves into ideological holes from which they cannot climb out. It was intellectuals-turned-politicians who got us into Vietnam and, with the help of two presidents, kept us there long after it was clear we should have got out.

The Ideological Demon, then, in his most pure and rarefied form appeals principally to intellectuals and to college students when they are going through their intellectual phase—that is to say, when the main adult models in their lives are faculty members. The number of potential ideologues in the country has risen in direct proportion to the increased number of college-educated and professional people. Most of those reading this book are probably more prone to the ideological temptation than are the masses of the American public. Still, the Ideological Demon knows that the public—or at least substantial segments of it—is available for ideological influence in times of crisis and uncertainty. He bides his time and waits.

But what is wrong with ideology? What is wrong with having systematic comprehensive analyses of social and political problems with a coherent and consistent set of responses to those problems?

What is wrong with it is that it is no damn good.

Why?

Because reality is far too complicated to be fit into any simple explanatory systems, nor can it be fit into any elaborate or complicated systems, either.

The systematic perspective is a useful tool for investigating reality, a helpful model for testing reality, perhaps even an indispensable chart for tentatively moving out into reality; but it cannot, of the nature of things, be either a description of reality or an adequate prescription for how to deal with reality. Even the most marvelously elaborate intellectual system is imperfect, limited, and ineffective as a description of the way things really are. The richness, heterogeneity, complexity of human, political, and social living cannot be squeezed into any intellectual system. It is too big, too elusive, too slippery, too sticky, too messy. Ideological temptation, like so many of those described in this book, is a revolt against the complexity, the rich, exciting messiness of the human condition. It is an attempt to reorder the world and the human race so that it will fit patterns of our design, not the patterns of whoever made it. Systems are useful and necessary scientific tactics; science abstracts from reality in order to understand portions of it. But politics cannot abstract from reality; politics take place right in the center of the messiest, murkiest, most complicated part of reality—where one human being encounters another. No system can ever explain that.

The only way to approach the messy interface between human beings is to be tentative, experimental, pragmatic, flexible. One must "play it by ear" or not play at all. What looks extraordinarily good on paper, in a textbook, or in a classroom may fail completely unless it is only a very tentative working hypothesis. When you get out into the world of emotion, passion, fear, hatred, and love you should expect nothing and everything.

The Ideological Demon abhors such a notion. He calls upon his allies the Gnostic Demon, the Scapegoat Demon, and the Ethnocentric Demon together to fight with him against it. An ideological system provides an analysis, a solution, a form of hidden knowledge, a list of culpable enemies, and a set of descriptions of these enemies to justify their elimination. Marxism is once again the quintessential ideology. The problem of society is the oppression of the working class. The solution is the seizure of power by that class—or at least by those members of the middle class who have identified with it. The enemies are the middle class (or those who have not identified with the worker's cause). (These days enemies are defined as "the Establishment," "the System," or "the Power Structure.") They are enemies because they are power hungry, corrupt, greedy. Ideology provides the secret knowledge that those with intellectual and moral superiority will free the oppressed ones and punish their enemies. Small wonder that when the Ideological Demon is hard at work, his colleagues rally around to help.

Beware then of the man who has all the answers. The only kind of person who can really make effective change in the real world is the one capable of questioning his own analyses and his own solutions, of showing some self-doubt about his list of answers he purveys in the market place of ideas.

Relatively little good has been done in the world by the grand theorists. Most of the improvement that has occurred in the human condition has been accomplished by sensible and pragmatic empirical men who have used the grand systems only when they have responded to the hunch, instinct, insight, and "feel" of a situation. It is to these men to whom the Pragmatic Angel speaks. "Try it," he says. "See if it works. If it doesn't work, get rid of it. If it does, push it a little further. Push until it stops working, and then try something else."

For the ideologue this style of approaching the human condition is appallingly sloppy. In addition it is probably immoral and corrupt. It is without principle; it shows the dangerous propensity to compromise; it is "eclectic."

The Church has had its share of ideologues in the last several decades. A certain kind of American Dominican thought he could find in the writings of St. Thomas Aquinas a description of and a solution for every conceivable human problem. Some of the enthusiasts of the early years of the Catholic action and

Catholic labor movements thought that papal encyclicals provided systematic blueprints for reconstruction of the social order.[5]

More recently the pop psychology movement in the Church
has provided a systematic religious explanation for everything in
the vocabulary of self-fulfillment and self-development. The impact of this movement is still very strong, and indeed it is probably the most influential intellectual or quasi-intellectual or
pseudo-intellectual stream of thought in American Catholicism
today. It filled the vacuum created when the old rigid apologetic
theological framework collapsed. No new theological vision has
been able to replace it. Psychology is fine, of course, but it is no
substitute for theology, and the present chaos of the American
Church is probably a sign of what happens when psychological
ideology replaces sound theology.

The Pentecostal movement—a recent sometime competitor,
sometime colleague of the pop psychology movement—also
shows strong ideological tendencies. Some of the Pentecostals, at
any rate, have both an analysis of and solutions for all conceivable human religious problems.

Ideology makes life easier. It dispenses one from the necessity
of thinking through the contingencies of a given situation; one
simply falls back onto one's system for both analysis and response. The elegance of the intellectual elaboration of ideological systems is both a disguise and a pretext for intellectual laziness. One can rely on the analysis of others rather than having to
do analysis for oneself in the concrete circumstances in which
one exists. The system provides a ready-made explanation for
failure (America wasn't ready for George McGovern); one never
has to consider the possibility that the system has blinded one to
reality rather than illuminating it.

The real world of human beings and political and social interaction responds slowly and grudgingly, and at that only to the

[5] To some extent this reliance on papal word was a cover for economic and
sociological naïveté. To some extent it was a club to force bishops into line,
and to some extent it was a moral argument to appeal for lay support.

person who respects its complexity. Surely the one who tries to stretch it and distort it to fit his preconceived scheme meets only resistance and futility.

The latest outburst of ideology in the Church is the so-called "third world theology." It is usually a mixture of vulgar Marxism and inferior theology. The "third world" theologian, self-proclaimed spokesman for the "victims" and the "oppressed," insists that Europeans and North Americans listen to them and take instruction from them, since those whom they represent cannot speak for themselves. Alas, all too many succumb to this moral blackmail and pretend that this strange mixture of vulgar Marxism and superficial Christianity—quite devoid of any economic and social scientific sophistication—is serious theology. They also seem to accept the ludicrous proposition that the proponents of this theology, usually well-fed professors ensconced in the comfortable life of the university, are indeed victims themselves.[6]

There is some reason to believe that economic growth in Latin America—an essential precondition for the improvement of the lot of its peoples—can occur only under the government of an oppressive police state. But whether that state be of the so-called Marxist variety, as in Cuba, or the so-called right wing variety, as in Brazil, seems to be less important than that it have the will and the ruthlessness to impose order and system on social structures that are too weak and fragile to sustain economic growth in a democratic polity. It may be great fun for Latin American intellectuals—theologians or not—to blame the United States and American imperialism for the economic plight of their countries. Certainly the record of the United States has been neither progressive nor admirable, but there seems to be no persuasive argument that the solution to the economic and political problems of these countries can be achieved by anything that Washington

[6] I except from this denunciation the Uruguayan writer Juan Luis Segundo. His series, *Theology for the Partisans of a New Humanity,* is a first-rate exercise in pastoral theology. But Segundo does not claim to be a theologian of revolution or of liberation or of the third world, merely a Christian theologian.

decides to do or not to do. This is a harsh truth, and if I were a Latin American theologian I might be reluctant to face it and even more reluctant to say it. Still, as a representative of a church which has made a god-awful mess of its ministry in Latin America for several centuries, I would be most reluctant to engage in moral blackmail of others. But then, pragmatic Chicago Irishman that I am, I am incapable of espousing an ideology and can't stand ideologues.

It ill behooves me to tell Latin American churchmen and theologians what they ought to do, although I doubt that any good will come from their flirtation with Marxism—as the Chilean disaster ought to have demonstrated conclusively. I further doubt that their religious and political analysis would be heard either by economic sophisticates or by the more pragmatic, flexible, and empirical approach to social problems.

But I can speak about American Catholicism. We have broken away only too recently from the rigid, controlled, a priori, deductive world of the Tridentine Church. I hope we experiment, at least for a while, with a tentative, exploratory, inductive, a posteriori approach to reality, which has been the genius of American Catholic politicians and in some ways the organizational genius of the American Church. When we were establishing ourselves as an organization, we listened with sweet and agreeable reasonableness to the Pragmatic Angel. But when it comes to our theories and to our answers to social and political and human problems we, as churchmen and ecclesiastical thinkers (lay and clerical), have been dutiful servants of the Ideological Demon.

It has been a hell of a combination.

CHAPTER 14

The Disillusionment Demon and the Angel of Enthusiasm

Life is hard. It is a struggle. The fertilized ovum will not automatically find a resting place on the walls of the uterus. Once implanted it will not necessarily grow to viability. It must struggle to be born, and once it is born it must struggle to breathe and to stay alive. In most times and in most places the life of a newborn human is short, nasty, and brutish. The child must struggle to grow up; an adult must struggle to achieve, to stay alive, to protect itself, to delay death.

All of us must struggle to break through the barriers that separate us from those we love. It is a fight to overcome indifference and inertia, fear and suspicion. It is a fight to build a better world, to reduce anxiety, hatred, infidelity; a fight to raise our children and to protect them from the harmful forces around them. There is never a moment's rest. The memorial inscription of the dead being at peace is not just a euphemism. Peace comes to the human creature not as with other creatures in a full belly and a secure nest; it comes to the human only with death.

Most of us die exhausted. It is not merely from old age and the weakening of our bodily resources but from weariness and the weakening of our emotional, spiritual, and moral resources. There has been too much effort; we tried too hard, and we are totally exhausted.

Most human efforts end in failure, most of what we try doesn't work, most human dreams are blighted; most human activity, as Gustave Weigel once remarked, given sufficient time goes badly.

The temptation is to give up, to stop trying, to live from day to day and let everything else slide.

To kill the pain of human existence, we deaden our perceptions, we moderate our dreams, we dampen the fires of our passion, we cut off our fantasies. Occasionally we permit ourselves some pleasure, but we do not ever get too deeply involved, for if we enjoyed it too much, the disappointment at its ending would be unbearable. We elect to "play it cool."

"Playing it cool" does seem a safe way to live. We minimize our involvements, political, occupational, interpersonal, religious. We do enough to get by, perhaps a little more for safety's sake, but the rest of the time we are disengaged. We imitate and caricature Eastern mysticism, seeking Nirvana (and a pseudo-Nirvana at that) here on earth.

Few of us are explicit about this engagement; few of us are cynical enough to admit that it is not worth it to try anymore. Few of us have so armored ourselves against the seductions of the Enthusiastic Angel that we are incapable of moments of excitement. Still there is a strong tendency in our lives toward disengagement, a strong propensity to minimize our involvement. The less we have to do the better. A can of beer, the television set, the latest issue of *Playboy* or *Good Housekeeping*, or, for some of us, occasional grass or extramarital sex—that's what life is all about.

There is much to be said for living that way, and the Disillusionment Angel has been telling us that for a very long time. We diminish our vulnerability, we limit our capacity for pain by removing ourselves from those areas of feeling and caring where the pain and vulnerability lurk. We might not get much done, but then nothing we do works anyhow, and this way we don't get hurt. The only time such an existence is disturbing is when we pause to ask ourselves what we have done with our lives. The Disillusionment Demon does his best to see that we don't ask that question too often.

There is a profound religious and theological issue at stake in the conflict between the Disillusionment Demon and the Enthusiastic Angel. It is an issue that most of us struggle with in the middle years of life. In fact, the "crisis of the middle years," which we have been hearing about lately, is fundamentally one of enthusiasm versus disillusionment. It is not very difficult to be enthusiastic in your twenties or even in your early thirties. You had fewer shattering experiences, and the various fluids in your organism flowed free and clear. But in the middle years the physical organism begins to wind down, the psychic organism flames out, and from that point on enthusiasm is less a matter of natural energy and more a matter of deliberate, conscious effort. The issue, quite bluntly, is whether it's worth trying or not. Since nothing I do can possibly matter, we say, why should I bother?

Jesus, of course, had something quite different to say. For us to turn away from the natural enervation of the aging organism may take a blind and heroic leap of faith. The Angel of Enthusiasm demands that we be ready to start over again, which is one of the most difficult things in all the world to do.

It means that each new morning, when we trudge to the job, we make a new beginning. Each first encounter of the day with the children is a fresh start. Each school year is a new opportunity. Each new group to come into a parish organization is a challenge. Each new person encountered is a fascinating new mystery. Each new episode of love-making is a chance to seek new pleasure. Each ring of the telephone or the doorbell is a chance for an interesting new development in our lives.

The Enthusiastic Angel is an angel of new beginnings, of starting over again, of rebirth, getting back on our feet after resurrection. Indeed, the Enthusiastic Angel is one of resurrection; he it was who sat in the tomb and waited for the apostles.

The rhythm of life is one of death and rebirth, burial and resurrection, of ending and beginning, of closing down and opening up, of bringing things to a halt and of starting over again. We stop being reborn only when we stop wanting to. Resurrection is impossible without enthusiasm, and it is the possibility of resurrection that excites enthusiasm. To quit, to give up, is to die; to try again, to start over, is to live. We rise from the dead only because we want to. And the only barrier to resurrection is quitting. "Disillusionment," as T. S. Eliot puts it in *The Cocktail Party*, "if persisted in is the ultimate illusion."

The Disillusionment Demon, then, is a spook, a ghost, an ephemeral bit of ectoplasm who claims for himself all the solid reality of a mountain, but if you look at him closely you can see right through him to the rising sun, whose rays reflect brightly off the shining wings of the Holy Spirit.

It is the best way to live, the only way to live. The world may be a random, capricious, absurd place; life may be a cruel joke; but even if it is, as the existentialists tell us, we must live in such a way that, if oblivion is our end, it is an unjust end imposed on us from the outside, not something we freely choose by default. Even if there is no purpose in our efforts, we must live as though there is lest our lives become as monotonous as the summer reruns on TV.

Of course, if we are creatures so designed that we must live with enthusiasm if we are to live at all, then that fact may say something about the design of the universe and the powers that are responsible for the design. In his indefatigable capacity for enthusiasm, his capacity to be reborn no matter how much of a beating he has taken, his ability to land on his feet no matter what he has been through may be one of the best hints we have of what life is all about. It is only a hint, of course, not an explanation, but it is all we have. What we make of these hints depends on our own courage and faith.

But how do we win the battle between enthusiasm and disillusionment that rages inside our personalities? It is very difficult to win it alone. Indeed, only the most extraordinary person can sustain his enthusiasm without social support. For most people the principal ally in the battle against disillusionment is their spouse, their most intimate friend, the one with whom, theoretically at least, they share the most. Indeed, if husband and wife are not mutually reinforcing and supporting one another's enthusiasm, it is very difficult to see how either can avoid succumbing to the Disillusionment Demon. There is great risk in challenging your mate to enthusiasm, because, inevitably, the challenge will come back. Unfortunately, in many marriages the rhythm is off the beat; instead of sustaining and reinforcing each other's enthusiasm they do their best to cancel the notes of enthusiasm as they appear. To switch the metaphor, they dump ice cold water on the sparks of energy and hope as soon as they start to catch fire. Things are much better between husband and wife, argues the Disillusionment Demon, if both of them play it cool and each makes sure that the other never stops playing it that way. There is no telling how much trouble they will get themselves into if they don't keep things quiet without excitement or enthusiasm. A little bit of excitement and enthusiasm may be all right when you're young, but later? Don't be silly. Act your age.

For priests and religious their communities or their colleagues should provide the support they need for sustaining enthusiasm. The only reason for having religious orders, it seems to me, is to guarantee that support and encouragement they need when their hope and excitement and their enthusiasm wane, and when the awful agony of having to be born again, to begin again, seems too much to endure.

But all too frequently religious communities and presbyteriates of the diocesan priests operate in exactly the opposite way. Far from generating enthusiasm, they quench it; far from offering support, they impose restriction and control; far from challenging us to rebirth, they urge us to settle down and not rock the boat. The vivid enthusiasm of the founder has been reduced to a code, to a set of slogans, to ritual formulae and prescriptions. His words are mouthed, his spirit ignored. Indeed, should he present himself in the community recreation room he would run the risk of being cut to ribbons. For it is the nature of those who founded religious communities that they were people who rocked boats. That is a very dangerous way to live; you can get comfortably adjusted in your place in the boat, and even if you don't get seasick, it can be uncomfortable to be forced to look at things from a different perspective.

The last thing in the world the Disillusionment Demon wants

is that the routine be disturbed, and rocking boats interferes with routine very definitely. Routine is absolutely deadly to enthusiasm. Once we have our lives organized so that we know exactly what we are going to be doing every day, week, month, year, there is no room left for enthusiasm. Who needs it? It will make us think, re-evaluate, reconsider, reorganize, and consider the possibility of rebirth. That's fine when you're young, but when you are older metanoia is a drag.

Spouses, communities—who else can we look to for encouragement to fight the Disillusionment Demon?

Ex officio, this is what we have religious leaders for. Whether he be a witch doctor in Africa, a monk in Tibet, a missionary in New Guinea, a shaman in Alaska, or a monsignor in the west of Ireland, the religious leader exists to comfort and to challenge. He earns a living; he gets paid for stirring up enthusiasm, for reassuring, encouraging, demanding, exhorting. It is his job to exorcise the Demon of Disillusionment. Even if he doesn't feel very enthusiastic himself, his job still demands that he excite enthusiasm in others. Even if he is quite prepared to sell his own soul to the Disillusionment Demon, still he must lead the battle against him.

When a priest or any other religious leader becomes cynical, turned off, sour, disillusioned, he is not earning his keep. He is no good to himself, surely, which may be his prerogative, but he is also no good to those who have hired him, and that is not his prerogative. He who is the salt of the earth and has lost his savor is good for nothing and should be cast out. He may well remonstrate that he never realized he was recruited to be the salt of the earth, to be the maestro of enthusiasm, to be the Vice President in Charge of New Beginnings. Such may well be the case, but one is forced to wonder what in the hell he did think he was being hired to do. But if he took the job with a misunderstanding of what it was all about, the honest thing for him to do is to get out or to settle down to the difficult task of fighting disillusionment whenever it occurs and encouraging enthusiasm whenever he sniffs the slightest whiff of its presence. That is what being a priest is all about. Indeed that is what being a religious leader in any time or any place is all about.

As long as humans are liable to disillusionment and as long as they are capable of enthusiasm, as long as life is caught in the rhythm of life, death, and rebirth, there will be a need for religious leaders. The clergyman who thinks that his mission is no longer relevant betrays his misunderstanding of both his mission and the nature of the human condition.

There are, of course, others besides the clergy (and I use the term in a broad sense to include women religious leaders as well as men) who are competent at fueling the fires of enthusiasm. Indeed, there are many who are better at it by natural talent and by personal effort than most of us are. But the whole point of having a clergy is not to leave to random chance the arrival on the scene of enthusiasts. The clergy exists precisely as an institutionalization of enthusiasm. They are there so that when people need help against disillusionment—and they may need it without even wanting it—that help will be available.

In fact that is what vocation is all about. One who does not want to exercise such a vocation, or thinks he is incapable of it might well be excused from it. But he should not be taken seriously if he argues that there is no point nor purpose nor excitement nor opportunity in such a vocation.

Even revolutionaries, Peter Berger has said, have to sleep; and enthusiasts, too, have restless nights, are harassed beyond endurance by the doorbell and the telephone. They have bad days, and periods of gloom and doubt. They need long, quiet vacations, too; and while the enthusiasm to which we are called is a glorious ideal, like all ideals we rarely come close to achieving them. But the Angel of Enthusiasm is precisely the one who has the responsibility of urging us to keep trying.

There is a voice across the river who is calling to us. Who is that voice? What is he calling? Where does he want us to go? That is the great mystery of human life, and the only way we will find out is to cross the river and see.

CHAPTER 15

The Pride Demon and the
Angel of Self-Respect

There are two chief demons presiding over all the others. The vice regent is Pride, and his master is Fear. When the other demons find the going tough, they appeal to one or the other or both of these. And both top brass demons are masters at disguising themselves.

The Pride Demon really deals in self-hatred, but he has very cleverly pretended that self-hatred masquerading as humility is the exact opposite of pride. In fact, pride and self-hatred are merely opposite sides of the same coin. Pride is the confident, haughty exterior that self-hatred puts on in order to hide its ugliness.

Envy, alienation, righteousness, inflexibility, rigidity, ethnocentrism, ideology are all the armor plates that the weak, insecure ego builds up around itself to provide protection against the assaults of a hostile world. They exist merely to conceal self-hatred. A person who is really convinced at the core of his personality that he has value, worth, and dignity does not need pride; he does not need all the protections that the proud person eagerly seeks and which the demons so readily provide.

It is sensible to protect oneself. While it is true that most people's personalities are remarkably tough and resilient, no one is unbreakable. We do not hand ourselves over to everyone who comes down the turnpike; we cannot trust everyone we encounter who seeks intimacy with us; we do not reveal who and what we are in the core of our beings to everyone who announces that he wants our friendship. Just as we do not promiscuously give our bodies to others, so we are sparing about whom we trust ourselves with too. Exhibitionism, either physical or psychological, is not a virtue.

Every human has his fragilities and vulnerabilities. He can get hurt. Most of us grew up in circumstances in which our self-confidence was damaged, or at least its development was inhibited. For good reasons (or so they thought or claimed) those responsible for our maturation process did not want us to "get bigheaded." They were afraid that if we became too self-confident we might do injury to ourselves, so they systematically allowed us to get hurt. Unfortunately internalized hurts render us no less vulnerable to further pain, so to avoid it we ward off intimacy and become wary and suspicious and closed up, feeling worthless and unworthy withal.

And this is just what the Pride Demon wants.

Self-hatred is a pathological fear of worthlessness. It is widespread, indeed almost endemic, in the population. I have frequently thought that it may be more prevalent in women than in men, because in our culture attractiveness is so important for women. But then it is possible that men are able to hide their feelings of worthlessness more easily by committing themselves more aggressively to the pursuit of occupational success. Of course self-hatred focuses on precisely those characteristics that society considers most important. The American male, no matter how successful he may be, is never successful enough. An American woman, no matter how lovely she may be, is never quite beautiful enough, or a good enough housekeeper, or a good enough wife or mother, or, in the world of feminism, a good enough competitor.[1]

Self-hatred is the result of radically conditioned love. It comes from childhood experiences in which we experience love only when we perform and have it withdrawn when we do not per-

[1] I am impressed that the feminist movement pays only occasional lip service to androgyny. For all practical purposes it seems to insist that women should become more like men, and show little concern that men acquire those traits society has chosen to define as "feminine."

form. Conditioned love is not merely a parent's growing angry at a child who has done something wrong or is a pest for an hour every day. On the contrary, anger and conflict between child and parent are healthy so long as they are out in the open. Conditioned love is something deeper than that. It is a feeling the child gets, absorbing it largely from the parent who is sending out the signal, that love has to be earned, purchased. The child discovers that he is not lovable for who and what he is but only for what he is able to do. If he doesn't do what the parent wants, the parent will withdraw his total regard for him as a human being. The bottom falls out of his universe.

In order to avoid such a traumatically painful experience the child learns quickly how to perform, how to keep the parent happy, how to earn love and keep it. But if you have to earn love, you have no sense of being worth loving for yourself; if you have to merit your parent's affection by your deeds, then it follows that there is nothing about yourself that is worth affection.

Conditioned love is a marvelously effective way of controlling a child, and it may be good training for existing in a competitive society. It is not, however, the way to raise a confident, self-possessed, self-respecting adult human being. Sometimes one gets the impression that many parents do not want that kind of a child growing up in their family. They would not know what to do with him.

The same approach to self-worth permeates the Puritan, Jansenist strain of the Christian religious tradition. The gospel is overwhelmingly clear to the point that God's love is unconditioned; His rain falls on the just and the unjust alike. He loves us without reservation, whether we merit it or not, whether we exert any effort to gain it or not. He initiates the dialogue of love. The issue is not whether we have earned it but whether we respond.

But while this theme is self-evident in the New Testament, still much of our religious life has been based on the premise that we have to earn God's affection by constant effort and striving. If we do not work hard at it, somehow or the other we will either not win His love or will lose it. God ends up as a touchy parent ready to withdraw love almost at the drop of a hat. Small wonder that those who have already experienced conditioned love in their childhood resent a God who plays the game the same way his parents did. To present God as someone who offers only rigid, conditioned love is one of the great diabolic successes of human history.

So the victim of conditioned love must *prove* himself in his family and in his religion, in school and in his personal relationships, his job and his life-style, and in his sexual conquests.[2] Everything that happens in his life is a new test, and he feels compelled to be top scorer. Challenge and opportunity are not something he enjoys, but something to be feared. He may fail, and failure for him is a disaster. He is not able to take his losses and get out and begin again somewhere else. Failure is not just an incident; it is a threat to the very core of his being. He therefore needs an immense collection of defenses to protect himself, to explain his failures when they occur, and to minimize the number of situations where failure is possible. The whole horde of fiends come rushing to his assistance to provide him with armor plating so thick that nothing much can ever hurt him again. But like the medieval knight who preferred the immobility imposed by heavy armor to the risks incurred by light armoring, the well-protected, proud, self-hating man has no mobility left; he is safe, but he cannot respond to anyone or anything. It is the safety of the tomb.

[2] Some of the recent research done by serious scholars on the so-called "swinging" subculture ("swinging," for the uninitiated, is spouse-swapping) have argued persuasively that swinging is something that a kind of insecure, upper-middle-class suburban man imposes on his wife in order that he may indulge in adolescent fantasies about his prowess as a lover without losing the comfort and convenience of a marriage. According to this literature, wives go along in part because they want to please their husbands and in part because it may also reassure them of their own attractiveness. Still swinging, while it may masquerade as liberated, progressive, advanced behavior, is in fact in most instances pure male chauvinism. It gives the insecure man the excitement of sexual adventure with none of its consequent dangers. But he enjoys his little adventure through the exploitation of his wife.

The well-insulated, proud person may not actually admit even to himself his fear of worthlessness, although an astonishing number of human beings will concede under the influence of an unguarded moment (or copious amounts of John Barleycorn) how little regard or respect they have for themselves. But the ultimate diabolic insulation against human pain and intimacy and life itself is so effective that the self-hating person never realizes he has the problem. He may think of himself as reserved or self-controlled, by temperament a loner; but his belief in his ability to live totally by himself is only a reflection of his need to insulate himself from pain; no one can ever hurt him again.

The fear of being known, of being seen for what one is, is the fear of death. Shame is a demon that affects everyone, but when self-hatred and pride are powerful, shame runs amok and assumes the guise of a particularly nasty kind of arrogance. When one encounters someone who seems obsessed by the need to criticize others and to pick, pick, pick away at the faults and failings of those to whom he is supposed to be close, then one has found a blend of shame and pride that is probably incurable. Such a person is so ashamed of who and what he is, so afraid of being known by others that it is not enough to cut oneself off from others; it is necessary to attack them with barbed darts before they get close.

The proud person can give himself to no one because he is quite incapable of trust. He is so convinced (albeit unconsciously, perhaps) of his utter worthlessness that he knows he would be destroyed in any intimate relationship. Life becomes a game, though a deadly serious one. One enters many relationships, because of course you must have relationships if you are to live, but the victim of self-hatred will insulate himself against intimacy and systematically attack to keep the other person at bay. Spouses, children, colleagues, friends are demolished or driven off—usually in such a way that the blame seems to be theirs. No one is permitted close to the real self, because he is afraid to reveal that there is no self. Pride is an act so convincing that the proud person sells it to himself and to the rest of the world. He is afraid and ashamed of his worthlessness, and he sets about punishing others in part because "others" are responsible for his worthlessness, in part to keep them at bay, and in part because he is steeped in guilt and needs to punish himself. (Alcoholism, the disease of the proud and the weak person, is a marvelous way of punishing yourself through others.)

It is a hellish life. The self-hating person has sealed off everyone else and attacks them when they get too close. The angels of light never have a chance; the Lord God himself has been excluded as much as anyone. The proud person has put himself in hell, and the demons of that place are delighted to see him there. That Adam and Eve and Satan committed sins of pride is absolutely sound theology, for it is pride (here understood as self-hatred) that cuts humankind off from the love of God. Pride renders God's love inoperative by making it radically impossible for the proud person to begin to respond. If he can just begin to respond, God will do the rest. The demons are ever watchful for the gleam of response that allows God's light to surge in.

The Angel of Self-Respect wars with the Pride Demon. I almost called him the Angel of Humility, but that word has been so sadly distorted by the machinations of the Pride Demon that I am reluctant to use it.

What is self-respect? Let me answer by quoting from a "faith biography" written by a sixteen-year-old high school junior. It is entitled "A Faith Autobiography." I reproduce it as she wrote it:

> Some people may say I'm too self confident; others may claim I'm basically insecure and it's all a cover up but as far back as I can remember I've held on to one belief that I've never changed. Even in my change of friends, schools and teachers this belief has never varied. I've always believed in myself.
>
> As a child, I was taught that I was special, unique, no one else was like me. I was taught to develop the talents I Possessed and if I really had a deep desire to do something, make something or be something, I could. I was capable of doing it.
>
> This belief in myself is the basis of my belief in anything.

The fact that I was taught I was something special and unique, I needed something or someone to thank, to explain why I was the way I was.

This is where my belief in God came from. God made me, so he understood me and had faith in me. When my faith in myself started to falter, God helped me realize again what I was.

My belief in myself convinced me to have faith in mankind as a whole. I believe people are conceived with good qualities and talents because I believe I was. Probably the most disappointing thing for me is to see someone with talent who doesn't spread it because they have no purpose or reason to use their talents. I've always tried to give someone like this a purpose to develop their talents.

That's the extent of the so called "faiths" of my life so far. Anything else I once believed in was so small and unimportant that it never really impressed me much. I never had faith in those small beliefs. I consider myself lucky though, for strong faith in too many ideals makes one more vulnerable to let downs.

Needless to say, the teacher was shocked and horrified by the piece. The young woman was "proud," "arrogant," "stuck-up." Obviously you do not want someone like that in the classroom. It would be a good idea to cut her down to size. The teacher was wasting her time. The young woman was sophisticated enough to admit in the opening sentences that it might be "pride," which of course is self-hatred, that led her to such a self-image, but those who know her have little doubt that her confidence is authentic and not a sham. She really did grow up believing she was someone special; and she was indeed special (as is everyone). She will go through life being someone special (and scaring hell out of all the proud people she encounters).

In a religious atmosphere in which humility has been perverted to mean "self-degradation," such a description of one's own personality is totally unacceptable. But in a religious atmosphere where it is believed that God has made each one of us "special" and worth an infinite amount of love, the young woman's description is absolutely sound. Of course, if she talks about nothing else, one could legitimately suspect her of pride, for constant repetition of such self-evaluation would obviously be done not for our benefit but for hers and would be a kind of psychological "whistling in the dark." Modesty and good taste are not the same things as the phony humility of self-degradation.

I have always felt sympathetic with the athlete who has just worked a remarkable feat—say pitching a no-hitter or gaining 250 yards in a game. Obviously what he has done has been splendid, yet he must be very careful about how he acknowledges the plaudits of his admirers. First of all he needs others' help, and truth demands that he acknowledge this. Secondly, if he seems too cocky, the next time around his blocking may suddenly vanish into thin air. The mores of the athletic world demand that he play down the importance of individual accomplishment and pretend that it wasn't really all that important after all. Such is the culture of the game, and it is not likely to be changed. Still it is hard to pretend that a record-breaking feat was almost entirely the result of others' efforts. An occasional athlete like Muhammed Ali who breaks from the custom and proudly announces, "I'm the greatest!" seems authentic; yet he was ostracized by the sports world and its press. But whatever the cultural customs are for the expression of modesty, they should not be confused with self-degradation. He who gains 250 yards and really persuades himself that it is not a major achievement is not modest and humble, he's stupid. Anyone who constantly minimizes his own worth and dignity, uniqueness, and value is not modest or humble; he is proud, and he is also stupid. God made him "special," and if he does not recognize it he is foolish. What a terrible waste of divine time and energy—to turn out the marvelous thing that a human is and then have the person himself reject that marvel.

Self-respect is an absolutely essential prerequisite for intimacy. If you do not think you are worth giving, then you can't give yourself to someone else; nor can you accept that someone else as a gift to you. To accept him would be to give him an opportunity to see what you are, and that would be death. In the absence of some minimal attention to the message of the Angel of Self-Respect, intimacy cannot even begin.

But once enough self-respect has been generated to get beyond the appearance of intimacy to the substance of it, then intimacy begins to improve and enhance self-respect. For in *real*—as opposed to make-believe—intimacy, tenderness is automatically generated, and tenderness is the best medicine for self-respect and the best antidote for self-hatred that the angels ever produced.

No one can have too much tenderness. It is impossible to err by excess in giving tenderness and even more impossible to have a surfeit of it. We absorb tenderness like a marshland absorbs water. Even a little bit of it, the slightest touch of it, illumines our day, dispels rain clouds, darkness, dampness, and makes life warm, bright, and sunny. It costs the one who gives it absolutely nothing, and it is priceless to the one who receives it. It is the best currency there is for human relationships. Both supply and demand are inexhaustible. It is astonishing, then, that the human race has not just about drowned itself in tenderness.

But in fact we give tenderness out as though it were in short supply; we ration it, limit it, curtail it, restrict it. The whole trouble with tenderness is that, if one gives it to another, one must be willing to receive it in return. And while it is delightful, it does strip away our defenses. A kind word, a concerned voice, a gentle touch, and we become quite helpless. Tenderness is great, but the cost of being helplessly in the possession of another is too much to pay.

The proud man pretends that he does not need tenderness, that it is beneath him. In fact, however, he is afraid of tenderness. It is too much for him; it suggests that he might be worth something after all, and his whole elaborate system of diabolic defenses is unnecessary. If he is worthy of tenderness, then he is lovable and he must risk himself in the encounter of human intimacy. If he is capable of giving tenderness, then he has something to give that does not depend on performance, and there is no escape from the challenge of intimacy. The proud person refuses to give or to receive tenderness, for if he did there might be nothing left. Still as long as he is tempted by the prospect of being tender to someone else and can feel even the faintest tinge of weakness when someone tries to break through to him, then there is still hope for him. The Angel of Self-Respect still has a fighting chance.

It is astonishing that there is not more tenderness between husbands and wives. The possibilities for and the varieties of tenderness available to a man and woman who share the same bed are practically limitless. Physical and psychological forces within them strain toward tenderness and should be almost irresistible. To touch, to kiss, to caress—there is no reason in the world why such affection is limited to the quarter hour before intercourse begins. It can permeate an entire relationship. Yet the risks of creating an atmosphere of sustained tenderness around one's relationship seems to be very high. Tenderness demolishes defenses. Many men and women cannot imagine what life would be like were it not hedged in by a mutually constructed and supported system of defenses that keeps their relationship cool, controlled, and safe.

And so the human race does not drown in tenderness; rather it is awash in harshness, suspicion, distrust, antagonism, anger, vindictiveness. Well, at least we are safe from wallowing in pleasure and delight. Pride, it has been said, goeth before a fall. But in fact pride is the result of a fall, a primal fall in which a human person comes to believe that he is not someone special, that he is not the object of a unique and passionate love.

Jesus came to battle pride and to tell us that each of us is special and the object of a special love. Small wonder that he was crucified.

CHAPTER 16

The Fear Demon and the
Angel of Hope

The Prince of Darkness is fear.

It would be nice to be what all the angels say we should be. In our fantasy lives we enjoy thinking of ourselves as enthusiastic, erotic, tolerant, flexible, committed, wise, trusting. We can readily admit the attractiveness of those humans who possess the qualities to which we are urged by the angels. We are also aware that there are mysterious but quite powerful forces within our own personalities drawing us to the angelic qualities. On occasion all those qualities seem to be released and we are indeed "something else." In those few rare moments when the angels are free to work we are transformed into a brilliant, dazzling, enormously attractive person. We have some sense of who and what we are and of who and what we are capable of being. In just those few moments it really seems foolish and impossible to be anything else.

Let us not underestimate the powers of the angels. They have survived a long time against what must surely be considered enormous odds, and they have not been phased out of the human condition. The Forces of Light have had a hell of a time of it, but they are still around; the darkness has not extinguished them.

We know, at least in our clear-sighted moments, how ugly the demons are. We don't like them in others and we are ashamed of them in ourselves. When we give rein to the demonic in us we are neither happy nor content. Safety it may produce but little else.

Why, then, do not the angels win the battle? Why is stalemate the best to be had from their struggle? The answer is that when all the other demons are routed the Prince of Darkness himself takes over. The chief devil, the one in the presence of whom even Pride is a rank amateur, steps forth and reveals himself in full power. It has suited his purpose to pretend that Pride is chief, but in fact Fear is the principal demon. He is shown as such even in the theology of Genesis. Adam and Eve are afraid of what will happen to them if they are not like God. Satan is afraid of what will happen to him if he is not God's equal. Pride is Fear's deputy; Fear is at the root of everything that is evil.

It was fear against which Jesus preached principally. He insisted in almost every one of his parables on the need for confidence in God's love and joyous response to that love. The gospel was fundamentally a polemic against fear. We have done our best for two thousand years to hide that fact, but all we have to do is to pick up the New Testament and read it again to discover that Fear was the enemy Jesus fought, and Fear the enemy that killed him. But Fear was conquered in resurrection.

Perhaps the most critically important words in the New Testament were spoken to the frightened apostles on the lake at Galilee: "Be not afraid, oh you of little faith!" For in this dictum Jesus equates fear with infidelity. We are afraid because we do not believe that we can trust the fundamental goodness of the universe. If we take all the risks involved in responding to the angels, then Something Terrible will happen. It is a Terrible that is raw, primal, undefined. If we have the rude presumption to refuse to be afraid of the Cosmos, then it will rear up to destroy us in venomous anger. Stated that baldly, stripped of sophistication and the trappings of recent civilization, the proposition seems absurd. Yet that is the way in fact the overwhelming majority of the human race has always lived—afraid to tempt the malign powers that lurk in the Cosmos. Jesus came to tell us that powers of benignity were infinitely stronger than malign ones. All we had to do was to believe in the benign power of the universe and we could conquer evil, sin, and death. "Too presumptuous, too much risk, crazy," his contemporaries said. And while we may credit with our lips his words, with our hearts we are still profoundly suspicious.

The Fear Demon urges us to caution and to conservatism. He cloaks himself thereby in an aura of responsibility and morality. Caution, conservatism are always more "moral," more "responsible," more "sensible," "prudent" than gambling, risk-taking. To live as though there was nothing ultimately to be afraid of would be reckless, irresponsible. To go along with the angels is to be radical, foolhardy, dangerous. To be what the angels want us to be would be to make ourselves vulnerable to a thousand injuries. It would be wildly, madly imprudent.

On the other hand, to live the life to which we are urged by the Angel of Hope opens us up to possibilities. It is exciting, breath-taking; but the roller coaster existence it promises is too scary. We settle for Fear.

The chief of all the angels is Hope. Indeed, he is not an angel at all, he is God's Holy Spirit. He is frivolous and reckless, a whirling, twirling, wheeling, dealing spirit of variety, laughter, joy, expectation. It is best to avoid him, because heaven only knows what will happen if we permit ourselves to be caught up in his lunatic dance.

Poets have strange, reckless ways of speaking to the Holy Spirit. Gerard Manley Hopkins, with some considerable historical tradition behind him, portrays the Spirit as a bird, brooding over the world with bent neck and bright wings. Francis Thompson sees him as a hound dog, relentlessly pursuing his prey. Nancy McCready portrays him as a haunt—but a merry one—a poltergeist, a playful spirit. Such lighthearted irreverence, we say. Cute, but hardly serious. That's not the way things are; least of all is it a proper, theologically accurate way to talk about the third person of the Most Blessed Trinity.

But in fact, if the message of Jesus is true, it is the way things really are, and it is an extremely appropriate way of talking about the Angel of Hope, the Spirit who speaks to our spirit, the flashing tongues of fire, the howling wind. What, after all, are these but an attempt to startle, seduce, inveigle us out of our dull, depressed, unhopeful, unfaithful, complacent routine?

The Angel of Hope really is a laughing, merry spirit. He really is a prankster, playing on us the greatest joke of all, and we call it Life.

We were taught, in the dear, dim, dead days before the Vatican Council, that hope had to do with our eternal salvation in the next life, and only applied in this life to things that were necessary for our salvation in the next. It was rather hard, of course, to reconcile such a vision of things with the gospel, because Jesus' vision of hopefulness seemed much more comprehensive, and Jesus seemed very much concerned with what happened in this life.

Hope encompasses much more than "eternal salvation." The distinction between "this life" and the "next life" is artificial; surely Jesus never made it. Hope has to do with life, and life is one. Hope does indeed imply resurrection; it indeed suggests that death is not the end but a change. But it makes the suggestion as part of a far more comprehensive vision of the meaning of life and the cosmos. Hope assures us that in the final analysis the cosmos is good. Life has meaning and purpose. At the core of the universe is passionate love. If such be the case, then we need not worry about risk-taking; we need not worry about survival. In fact, we need not worry about anything except living to the fullest. The Angel of Hope tells us that God is not only good but, you damn fools, He is wild; and only a life of wild hopefulness responds to things the Way They Really Are.

Our response is to concede that this is a distinct possibility. That there is goodness, mysterious but powerful goodness, on the loose in the cosmos and in the human personality is undeniable. The question is how far ought we to trust this goodness? The answer most people work out is the "agnostic compromise" (though not everyone willingly appends the word "agnostic" to compromise").

One version of the agnostic compromise says that life is good, the universe is benign. But it is not absolutely good, indeed, not sufficiently good to underwrite the survival of human life and the constant taking of risks. Life has purpose, the agnostic guesses, but he is not sure what it is. Life is good, he concedes, but only up to a point. He cannot see beyond to a point where good is stronger than evil. One must therefore vigorously assert the goodness of life, and live as goodly a life as possible, but the conviction remains that it may all be a meaningless absurdity between two oblivions.

Undoubtedly some people can live that way—mostly because they have internalized the habits of the Christian tradition in their early childhood and can live that tradition while professing not to believe it. But most humans are not capable of sustaining lives of generosity, trust, openness, and commitment unless they have some basic conviction about whether these things matter. As the theologian John Cobb has put it: "Life matters only if it matters ultimately. And it matters ultimately if it matters everlastingly."

If the agnostic compromise makes it impossible to live a life of Christian hope, following the dancing spirit of Hope, it also makes it impossible to live a life of hedonistic, pagan despair. The agnostic is neither hot nor cold, he is a heathen like G. K. Chesterton's friend Higgins.

The Song of the Strange Ascetic

If I had been a Heathen,
  I'd have praised the purple vine,
My slaves would dig the vineyards,
  And I would drink the wine;
But Higgins is a Heathen,
  And his slaves grow lean and grey,
That he may drink some tepid milk
  Exactly twice a day.

If I had been a Heathen,
  I'd have crowned Neæra's curls,
And filled my life with love affairs,
  My house with dancing girls;
But Higgins is a Heathen,

And to lecture rooms is forced,
Where his aunts, who are not married,
  Demand to be divorced.

If I had been a Heathen,
  I'd have sent my armies forth,
And dragged behind my chariots
  The Chieftains of the North.
But Higgins is a Heathen,
  And he drives the dreary quill,
To lend the poor that funny cash
  That makes them poorer still.

If I had been a Heathen,
  I'd have piled my pyre on high,
And in a great red whirlwind
  Gone roaring to the sky.
But Higgins is a Heathen,
  And a richer man than I;
And they put him in an oven,
  Just as if he were a pie.

Now who that runs can read it,
  The riddle that I write,
Of why this poor old sinner,
  Should sin without delight—
But I, I cannot read it
  (Although I run and run),
Of them that do not have the faith,
  And will not have the fun.[1]

The more sophisticated and urbane form of the agnostic compromise is that presented recently in the civilized and intelligent
religious journal, *Zygon*. This compromise vigorously asserts that
there is a God, but he is an inanimate force somehow identified
with all that is active and dynamic in the universe. Under the
influence of Alfred North Whitehead this compromise was even

[1] "The Song of the Strange Ascetic," The Collected Poems of G. K.
Chesterton. New York: Dodd, Mead & Company, 1941; pp. 199–200.

willing to concede that this force could be called Love. In fact, it could be conceded that God is Love.

But it is a rather peculiar kind of love. It does not care about those It loves. It is a love which is not superior to human love, which does indeed care about the love object. God, in other words, is not permitted certain admirable traits that humans have. Charles Hartshorne, a philosopher in Whitehead's mode, tells us that it is arrogant and selfish to be concerned about survival, and presumptuous to think that our relationship with the deity can be an everlasting love affair, one that death does not blot out.

Maybe. There is a sort of aloof, existential courage about this agnostic stance (which looked good when the Stoics advanced it a couple of millennia ago). It is not, I think, a courage open to most human beings, and it has precious little to do with Christianity. As to the question of whether hope or despair (which is, of course, just another name for fear) is appropriate when regarding human life, even this urbane and civil agnosticism will argue that there are grounds for "cosmic hope." But for me, a person, there is no hope at all. I may be absorbed into the Divine Consciousness, but the "I" that I know will no longer be. And if that is not despair, I don't know what is. If things really were that way, the best move would be to abandon the brave agnostic stoicism and seek for G.K.'s dancing girls.

The Demon of Fear tells us that the cosmos is a torture chamber filled with threats, dangers, pain, suffering, sorrow, anxiety. There is no escape; the best we can do is to tolerate it until oblivion kills the pain permanently.

The Angel of Hope tells us that the cosmos is a haunted house and that he is the haunt. We all know that haunted houses can be splendid fun especially if the ghost is a playful spirit, a prankster, a comedian.

A torture chamber or a house haunted by a comic spirit? The cosmos is one or the other. Our lives must ultimately follow the direction indicated by the Prince of Darkness called Fear or the prankster spirit called Hope.

You pays your money and you takes your choice.

CHAPTER 17

Angels We Have Heard on High

In the beginning of this book I argued strongly for the reality—if not the personality—of demons. Not only are there evil dispositions in our own personalities, there are mysterious evil forces beyond the personality that permeate both the social and physical worlds. These forces are pervasive, powerful, and almost—but not quite—irresistible. By ourselves we seem quite incapable of coping with them. Whether they are personified or not is much less important than that they are.

But I would really like to think that there are angels. I know that the Malek Yahweh of the Old Testament is really just a manifestation of Yahweh's power; it is not personified, save, perhaps, in the dimmest and vaguest way. I know that the angels of the intertestamental (or Second Temple) era were the result of the mixture of Platonic philosophy, Zoroastrian dualism and residual nature religions. Still, it would be nice if there were angels. I must admit that I find a certain attractiveness in the suggestion of one theologian that, since such beings are possible, it is likely they exist.

Nor am I alone in my hope that there are angels. A good deal of science fiction is written about beings of superior intelligence and ability that are afoot (or whatever they use for locomotion). If you are a *Star Trek* fan, they exist in other segments of the quadrant. Surely some of the creatures the crew of the *Enterprise* met in their all too brief explorations were quasi-angelic, as are many of the mysterious strangers that inhabit the world of science fiction.

For example, in the gripping novel *The Inferno,* by Fred Hoyle, the famous astrophysicist, and his son Geoffrey, a quasar erupts near earth and slowly begins to destroy all life. But suddenly a new force intervenes and begins to "turn off" the quasar:

Now he knew the explanation to be rational but not natural. He knew an intelligence, a creature, had intervened at their direst moment. It was as if a man should hold up a hand to shield the moth as it flew near a candle. The moth could not understand how or why it came to be saved, as Cameron had failed to understand how or why it came to be saved. Just as man was a creature of a different order to the moth, so a creature of a different order to man had intervened, intervened perhaps everywhere throughout the galaxy, intervened to protect the little creatures of the universe.[1]

All you have to do is to call the "creature" Gabriel and you have an angel on your hands.

The Hoyles discovered that there is good at work in the universe not only in our personalities but also in the social and the cosmic world. These forces of good are as powerful and as mysterious as the forces of evil (perhaps a bit more powerful and a little bit more mysterious). What matters is that the forces are. Whether they are personified, as we understand "person," is less important. There is a battle between angels and devils raging in the personality of each one of us. That battle between good and evil, between our generous, open, trusting, noble instincts and our frightened, anxious, closed, punitive instincts is merely our participation in a cosmic confrontation. We may pretend such a confrontation does not exist; we may argue that science has never been able to measure it. Still our instincts, our sensibilities, our poetic insights and intuitions leave little doubt that we are involved in something much bigger than ourselves.

Both the superstitious man and hyperrationalist man are deficient as human beings. The superstitious person (and he is still

[1] Fred Hoyle and Geoffrey Hoyle, *The Inferno.* New York: Harper & Row, 1973, p. 185.

in the majority in the human race, I think) believes rather little in scientific regularity and predictability. Everything that happens is the result of the intervention of good or evil spirits, good or bad magic. He is forced to think up an ad hoc explanation for everything that happens in his life.

The hyperrationalist, on the other hand, is deficient because he thinks (in disagreement with modern physics, incidentally) that regularity and predictability eliminate mystery and surprise from the cosmos. For the hyperrationalist the cosmic dance is the result of random chance. One has scientific predictability on the one hand and chance on the other, and that is what the world is all about.

But even those who intellectually accept such a position find it hard to live with, because *something* seems to be going on and we seem to be part of it. Once we get beyond the narrow rationalisms of a moribund positivism the issue is no longer whether there is a war in heaven but which side we are on.

Are we on the side of the angels? Have we allied ourselves with the forces of good in the universe? The honest answer for most of us, it is to be feared, is that we have decided to be neutral—benignly neutral perhaps, leaning to the side of Michael and his crowd, yet scarcely interested in getting involved. Michael and his commandos will have to go it alone pretty much. The available evidence would suggest that they are not having all that easy a time of it.

Still the blast of sound and light that is Christmas seems to suggest that the angels still have a few surprises up their sleeves. Surprise is the secret weapon of the angels; surprise keeps human beings open, and as long as they are open the angels still have a chance. The more we are capable of surprise and wonder, the more the angels are likely to arrive on the scene to disturb us. When our capacity for surprise is gone, the angels are gone too, and hell has begun.

Do I believe in angels and devils? Only a blind fool is unaware of the powers of good and evil and the conflict between them that fills our cosmos. Only a person totally lacking in self-awareness does not perceive this cosmic battle constantly reflected in his own personality; and only the dullest, most naïve, mundane of humans does not occasionally cock his ear to listen half expectantly for the sound of a trumpet.